GYPSY PREACHER

The author has identified as 'Gypsy Preacher' for over thirty years, reflecting his heritage and calling within the Romani community.

JOHN PURCELL

Dedication

To my late wife Patricia Purcell, a woman of great patience who spent countless hours repeating scriptures to help me memorise them. To our six children, our family circle, and my extended family in the Lord: where would I be without you and my Saviour.

GYPSY PREACHER

Copyright © 2025 John Purcell

Paperback ISBN: 978-1-915223-34-0

All rights reserved.

No part of this publication may be reproduced, stored in a retrieval system, or transmitted in any form or by any means, electronic, mechanical, photocopying or otherwise, without prior written consent of the publisher except as provided by under United Kingdom copyright law. Short extracts may be used for review purposes with credits given.

Main Bible Translation: New International Bible
THE HOLY BIBLE, NEW INTERNATIONAL VERSION®, NIV®
Copyright © 1973, 1978, 1984, 2011 by Biblica, Inc.® Used by permission. All rights reserved worldwide.

Other Bible Translations: New King James Version
Scripture taken from the New King James Version®. Copyright © 1982 by Thomas Nelson. Used by permission. All rights reserved.

Published by
Maurice Wylie Media
Your Inspirational & Christian Book Publisher

Publisher's statement: Throughout this book, the love for our God is such that whenever we refer to Him, we honour Him with capitals. On the other hand, when referring to the devil, we refuse to acknowledge him with any honour to the point of violating grammatical rule and withholding capitalisation.

Endorsements

Every once in a while, God brings someone across your path who makes a lasting impression on you. John Purcell (or Kevin, as we have always known him) is one of those people. I first met John at a barn mission, where he shared his testimony shortly after becoming a Christian. For John, becoming a Christian meant a completely new way of life for him and his family. By his lifestyle, his unique preaching ability and his wholehearted commitment to Christ, John has introduced many to his Saviour over the years that have passed since our first meeting.

I am privileged to consider John (and his late wife Patricia) and their family as fellow co-workers in the gospel.

This book will both inspire you and challenge you as you follow John's amazing journey of faith in Jesus!

David Bell,
Pastor, Mountain Lodge Pentecostal Church, Darkley, County Armagh.

I first came into contact with John almost 30 years ago, and like anyone who has ever met him, I will never forget that moment. I witnessed his compassion for people and his overwhelming love for our Lord.

Knowing his journey—from being a chief sinner to walking the Christian path—he is a true miracle, transformed from where he was to where he is today.

An international evangelist and elder in our church, I am honoured to call him my friend. If there were ever a Bible verse that perfectly describes my precious brother in Christ, it would be, "I have fought the good fight, I have finished the race, I have kept the faith." (2 Timothy 4:7-8).

Jacob Boyd,
Elder, Metropolitan Church, Newry, County Down.

A faithful witness to the transforming power of the Holy Spirit, a true servant of the Most High God, with a passion for souls to experience the abundant life, liberty, and joy found in Christ alone.

WJ Ervine
Pastor, Ava Street Pentecostal Church, Belfast.

Acknowledgements

Firstly, I give all honour and praise to my Lord and Saviour, Jesus Christ, for transforming my life and favouring me with the opportunity to preach the message of love, hope, and salvation. His grace has carried me, enabling me to minister to multitudes and win souls in many nations for His Kingdom. Over the years, numerous people have asked, "When will you be writing a book?" It's somewhat humorous, given that I can't read or write, so I knew that when the time was right, God would bring the right people along to help me.

With that in mind, I want to express my deepest gratitude to Paul and Angela for their unwavering support and encouragement throughout this journey of recording my story. God bless this hand-picked couple.

Special thanks to my publisher, Maurice Wylie Media, for believing in me and not viewing my reading or writing as obstacles. I commend the editorial team for their insightful input and expertise, which helped shape my story into this book.

Finally, I want to thank my friends and brothers in Christ for all your prayers and encouragement over the years. Each of you has played a role in my story.

John Purcell (Rev.)

Foreword

My wife, Shirley and I have known John Purcell and his family for over 20 years. I first met John at the former Annaghanoon Christian Ministries near Waringstown in Northern Ireland. We were staying at the small apartment attached to the hall, and after the meeting, we invited John and others to come up to the apartment for a cup of tea. I clearly remember trying to discern what kind of character this man was. His personality immediately made him the centre of attention, and his stories had us all captivated, each one carrying a gospel message.

Little did we realise that John, his late wife Patricia, and his children would become our close friends in the years ahead. At that time, I was a travelling preacher, working in the North of Scotland, the South of Ireland, and Northern Ireland. John was also a travelling evangelist, and our hearts were intertwined with a common bond: preaching the Gospel and leading people to the Lord Jesus Christ for salvation.

The Purcell family was gifted and talented. In the many Christian meetings they held, the children sang, Patricia recited poetry she had written, and John would preach. His sermons were straightforward, passionate, and powerful, always concluding with an altar call, inviting people to surrender their lives to Jesus and be born again. As people responded to the call of Christ, John was prepared to stay through the night, ministering to and counselling those who had responded. He would also pray for the healing of the sick and for the breaking of curses over individuals and families. Through their selfless ministry, the Purcell name became known nationally and internationally.

Testimonies of souls saved, people healed, and others set free through John's ministry can be heard throughout Ireland and beyond, including America and the Philippines. In Scotland, my native home, we often ministered together. It was the tent missions organised by the Perth Christian Fellowship, held throughout Scotland, that opened new doors for John. From the Orkney Isles in the north to the Scottish Borders in the south, John was a much sought-after preacher. His style, a mixture of humour and emotion, caught the attention of various congregations. He had a cutting edge that could penetrate the hardest of hearts and earned the respect of pastors and ministers from a variety of denominations, even those whose theology differed from John's beliefs—especially in his healing ministry. It is hard not to believe in healing when you witness someone being healed before your very eyes.

Patricia, his beloved wife and soulmate, passed away in 2021. She was the lynchpin of the ministry, organising events and keeping the diary up to date with places and dates where John was invited to preach and minister. As you will learn in this book, John only attended school for one day, leaving him unable to read or write. With help from Patricia, who had a spiritual anointing in her own right, he learned most of the Bible through her.

He has never lost his passion for souls and continues to minister wherever and whenever the opportunity arises. In writing this Foreword to John's book, my wife and I consider it a real honour and privilege to call John Purcell a valued friend and a precious brother in the Lord.

Pastor Donald Buchanan
Highways-Byways-Missions, Donaghcloney, Craigavon, Northern Ireland.

Contents

	Foreword 9
	Introduction 13
Chapter 1	Rain Hail and Hunger 15
Chapter 2	"Will You Marry Me?" 27
Chapter 3	Lost But Ignorant 37
Chapter 4	We Have Our Religion 45
Chapter 5	Homeward Bound 51
Chapter 6	Loving Through Gritted Teeth 61
Chapter 7	Discovering Life with a Wife 69
Chapter 8	The Day I Swapped Partners 77
Chapter 9	The Well Within 83
Chapter 10	Boundaries are Defeated in Christ 87
Chapter 11	Same Yesterday Today and Forever 103
Chapter 12	Caged or Not He is Worthy of Praise 119
Chapter 13	Kissing the Pig 125
Chapter 14	Discovering the Gift 133
Chapter 15	God is Calling 143
Chapter 16	Do You Meet the Requirements 149
	Contact 155

Introduction

The church was packed to the brim, every pew filled, even though it wasn't a Sunday. The congregation sat in eager anticipation, dressed in their finest suits and dresses. Aside from a few curious guests and travellers, most of the familiar faces—church members and their neighbours—knew exactly why they had gathered.

It was only two weeks prior that the pastor had eagerly announced that Reverend John Purcell, the founder and chairman of the Purcell Ministry, had agreed to visit as a guest preacher. Everyone was encouraged to attend the special service. Word of his visit travelled fast throughout the area, causing excitement. Those who had heard of Reverend Purcell but had never heard him preach, unwittingly, promoted the service by telling everyone he was coming. The date on calendars had been circled, and the focus was now set.

Talk around town was, "He's a great man of God, anointed to preach," or "A miracle worker." But in response to all these titles, Reverend Purcell's own words were more modest: "The greatest privilege is to love God and each other. I pray I may not be known for the miracles or my preaching, but as a vessel of love—God's love." As the scriptures say, *'Many will say to Me in that day, 'Lord, Lord, have we not prophesied in Your name, cast out demons in Your name, and done many wonders in Your name?'* (Matthew 7:22). And let us never forget, it is not what we say or what others hear about us that opens Heaven's gates— *'It is by their fruits you will know them.'* (Matthew 7:20).

As the day drew nearer, conversations buzzed with anticipation, and a sense of something extraordinary hung in the air. It was later remarked that crowd numbers never bothered him; the main goal was simply to be in the Lord's will.

After the usual proceedings at the start of the meeting, the pastor stepped forward, introducing their guest preacher with an air of solemn respect. He then invited Reverend Purcell to the pulpit. John walked onto the stage with quiet humility, but as he began to speak an unmistakable shift took place in the atmosphere. It was as if an unseen force filled the room. Every eye locked on him, and every ear attuned to his voice. A pin dropping could have echoed through the church.

This man was unlike the many eloquent preachers who could stir a crowd with their words, nor was he an entertainer who could win applause only to be forgotten when the lights dimmed. Reverend Purcell was something different—spirit-filled, losing himself entirely in the message he felt called to share. As he preached, it was as though he commanded a storm, letting it rage and then calming it, guiding his listeners through every swell and silence until his words sank deep into their hearts.

And then, something remarkable began to happen. The atmosphere grew thick with emotion as tears welled up in eyes and handkerchiefs appeared, attempting to wipe away what could not be held back. One moment, laughter rippled through the crowd as he shared a light-hearted story; the next, a profound silence fell as he delivered a piercing truth. For many, this was a new experience—they had never encountered such raw passion for Jesus, nor a preacher who could weave a simple tale into a life-changing lesson.

By the time Reverend Purcell finished, many in the congregation felt their hearts had been fundamentally altered, stirred to make pivotal decisions about their spiritual journeys. Yet, even as they left that night, few truly knew the man behind the message. They didn't notice that he never once opened his Bible. They hadn't glimpsed the childlike drawings hidden among its pages. They had no idea of his past—of the illiteracy he struggled with or the darkness he had overcome.

Now, we at Maurice Wylie Media are honoured to share with you the life and story of Reverend John Purcell, as he shared it with us—his words faithfully captured, each story meticulously recorded, and every detail reviewed by him to ensure its accuracy.

Let us introduce you to the extraordinary journey of the Reverend John Purcell.

Maurice Wylie Media

CHAPTER 1

Rain Hail and Hunger

I was born in The Coombe Hospital, Dublin, on November 22, 1946. Now, you might think my birth was a miracle—but the real miracle? That I wasn't kidnapped while I was in that hospital.

Back in '46, Ireland was a place where a baby's arrival was celebrated in a special way. Newborns were taken from their mothers, baptised, and then christened in the presence of the family—a moment to remember, where the baby's name would be joyously announced. But behind the joy and tradition, a darker secret loomed. Some priests, working in secret collusion with the local Garda, would scout these newborns. Under the cover of night, they would slip into the wards, gently lifting a few babies from their cots, wrapping them up, and handing them off to the waiting officers. The Garda, in turn, had connections to childless couples in America, Australia, and Europe—buyers who would pay handsomely for a baby.

It wasn't until later in life that I learnt from my parents just how close I came to being one of those babies, whisked away to a foreign land. Imagine me speaking with a Gypsy brogue, tinged with an Australian or American twang! People already struggle to understand me with my Newry, Liverpool, Gypsy accent—throw that into the mix, and they wouldn't stand a chance!

My daddy and mammy were the greatest parents any child could ever wish for. To me, Daddy was a role model. He was a caring provider who never hesitated to protect his family. If he wasn't around and danger was imminent, you could be sure our mammy would come running with a saucepan in her hand.

It is rumoured by a select that Gypsies would steal the eye out of your head, but that was never the life my parents raised us to lead. My dad showed by example how to live a good, responsible, and respectable life. He always wanted the best for his family and taught us to aim high and achieve the best we could. My mammy, on the other hand, played a vital role in raising us, caring for the children with love and dedication. Together, they were a perfect couple, working tirelessly to provide for us.

Although the South remained neutral during The Emergency—Ireland's term for World War II—it faced significant shortages in food, fuel, and other basic supplies due to wartime rationing. Many families in the city lived in poverty, and unemployment was high. Daily life in Dublin often revolved around traditional practices. For entertainment, our families gathered around the radio to listen to popular broadcasts; as for television[1] it would be introduced later to Ireland. Horse-drawn carts shared the streets with buses and bicycles, and the city had a modest but developing transport system. Corner shops and local markets were the main food sources, and due to rationing, people had to be resourceful with their meals. For us, being at the bottom of the pile, a decision was made: The Purcells were on the move to Liverpool, where a strong Irish travelling community resided.

We arrived at 18 Mulgrave Street, Liverpool, to the welcome of an Irish housewife. Standing on the street looking up at the height of the house, I smiled, as I couldn't believe we would have so much room to live in. That thought didn't last long.

---

[1] Television was officially introduced to Ireland on December 31, 1961, with the launch of Teilifís Éireann, which later became RTÉ (Raidió Teilifís Éireann).

She invited us all in and told us to follow her. We went up a set of stairs, and on the second landing, I noticed a cooker sitting there—not exactly the cleanest. In fact, nothing about it was clean, saucepans and all. I would later learn that this was our shared kitchen. A landing with a cooker.

She opened a door, and behold, I saw our accommodation all at once. It was a large room with a fire at one end and virtually no walkways; the room was crammed with beds. When we got any food, it was placed in plastic bags and hung on nails driven into the walls. It wasn't pleasant.

We were a tight family—so tight that even the dogs shared beds with us. The children would pile into several beds and fall asleep side by side. By morning, it was a sight to behold; a foot on your face, a few siblings lying on the floor after falling out of bed, and some sprawled over each other.

Let me share a wee secret about the winter nights. My brother was very close to our dog, and if you saw one, you saw the other. I always made sure my brother shared the bed with me and some of our other siblings. He'd jump into bed, with the dog following close behind. The blanket would cover them both, and I'd lie there pretending to sleep, watching him through slightly open eyes. When I knew he was fast asleep, I'd slide my hand down the bed, moving slowly so as not to wake him. Stretching my arm as far as I could, I'd catch the dog's tail and pull the dog up beside me. Nobody knew my "hot water bottle" had four legs.

Being the eldest of what would eventually become 13 boys and 5 girls in our family, responsibility fell upon me. An example of this was when our parents left for work. The landlady of the house would gather us up, and regardless of what we were wearing—shorts, nightdresses, or whatever—we were put out onto the street, rain, hail, or snow. It's funny how small memories from back then stick with you. I still remember her pushing us out of our room, down the stairs, and up the hallway to the front door. I would try to push back against her, hoping we could stay inside, if not for the heat, at least to stay dry. But a ten-year-old doesn't have the power of an adult, and out the door we went, with force, whether we liked it or not. Some of us fell into puddles, though it hardly mattered; within minutes, we were all soaked as we sought cover under a tree or shed to escape the rain.

We would stand there, hugging each other, trying to stay warm while our wet clothes dried on us. Then came the moment I dreaded each day… I'd hear, "I'm hungry" or "I'm thirsty." When those words came, it wasn't about what I wanted; it was about the love I had for my siblings. I would think, *What would Dad do?* The conclusion was simple: I had to step up and do what was right, and in this case, that meant finding food and drink for them.

But there was a problem—we had no money to buy food or drink. And with the rain pouring down, it was going to be a long, miserable day. So, I made a decision: I had to go and obtain food—a nicer way of saying… stealing.

Leaving the oldest sibling in charge of the others, I headed off, not knowing what the next couple of hours would have in store for me.

Getting the drink part sorted was easy. The milkman would leave fresh milk at the front doors of houses, and on my way back, whoever had failed to bring in their bottles would find them gone.

You should have seen my sisters' and brothers' faces when they spotted me coming up the hill, a bag full of pieces of bread in hand. Their excitement for that moment made them forget about the rain. Food was on the table—or in this case, a mucky floor in the park where we spent most of our days.

You might be wondering how I managed to get bread when I had no money. Well, I had a plan. I'd knock on doors and ask the person who answered, "Could I have some bread to feed the ducks in the park?" When they saw my wee innocent face, they usually handed over a slice or two. If I knocked on enough doors, I'd end up with enough slices to make a whole loaf.

And you know what was special about our loaf? It was a loaf you couldn't buy in a shop, made up of slices from numerous loaves: hard crust, soft crust, white bread, brown bread, hand-cut slices—no two the same thickness. To give it a bit of added colour, some pieces were even blue with mould! But hey, I could easily remove the blue bits.

Entrance to Princes Gate/Princes Park, where my siblings and I would seek shelter each day

When it came to education or pursuing knowledge as a student, I had no interest at all. Student life didn't appeal to me, and I never liked going to school. Therefore, I have no educational background and no qualifications whatsoever that I can proudly mention—except for the qualification I have in God. I can still vividly remember my first day at school. When I think back, I must have broken the school attendance record for the shortest time ever.

I'm not sure when the conversation took place between my dad and mum, but one thing I do know is that their plan for me and my plan were very different when it came to attending school.

When my mammy woke me up that morning, it was like any other day. Nobody told me I was going to school. Even then, I had no idea what a school or a student really meant. I only knew school as a place where young boys and girls went and then returned home after some time. Then I heard the bath water being poured from a saucepan that had been heated on the fire. I was slightly confused, as this was not bath day. But it wasn't long before my confusion cleared—the bath was for me..

When I came downstairs, all dressed in my finest clothes and smelling nice, my eyes nearly popped out of my head. There on the table was a large breakfast—all for me. *This day is getting better*, I thought. Then Dad came in and said, "Come, we have a journey to do!" Excited, I hopped into Dad's old, petrol-run lorry. I never realised until it was too late, but after a short drive, Dad pulled the lorry up beside a school. He jumped out through his door, shouting at me to "Com' on!" I jumped out after him, and he grabbed my hand, leading me up the school corridor and into a classroom.

This was a whole new world to me. As I stood there, the faces of little boys and girls—who looked like aliens—gazed at me. No one spoke.

Out of the corner of my eye, I noticed a large, imposing woman standing in front of a blackboard, teaching something to the students as we entered. Silence still filled the room as she reached out and took my hand, leading me to a small, empty seat. My dad exchanged some words with her, and I heard her say, "He will be alright; you can go." Dad then weaved his way out of the classroom and back to the parking lot to drive home.

As soon as I heard the engine of his lorry roar to life, I started to cry, "I want my daddy! I want my daddy!" The teacher rushed to my side, knelt beside me, and tried to calm me down. She patted my back and assured me that everything would be alright, saying many soothing words. But her efforts were in vain; I only cried louder and louder, "I want my daddy! I want my daddy…" Unstoppable tears fell on my desk and floor.

I kept on crying for what felt like a long time. Then, as if in answer to my desperate cries, my dad returned to the classroom. Bursting through the door, he told the teacher that the police had come with a notice to vacate the camp where our caravans were settled. The teacher stood aghast, lost for words, as my dad continued, "We are travelling to another location," and then he took me by my arm and together we left the classroom. I would never return.

Daddy's appearance in that classroom and the words he spoke to the teacher felt like the most magical rescue to a young boy who never wanted to be there. The Education Welfare Service never enquired about the incident or tried to bring me back to school. Once my parents realised I had no interest in attending, they never attempted to send me again. That marked the end of my school career, which lasted barely 30 minutes—a choice I still suffer the consequences of, including my inability to read and write.

Having completely abandoned school life, I grew up among other Gypsy kids who, like me, had either given up on education or never been to school at all. Together, we formed a motley group of young boys who loved freedom and lived carefree lives. We would go swimming, hunting, and fishing, without realising in our tender years that we were actually learning survival skills, preparing our young bodies and minds to face the challenges of adulthood. Sometimes, we would spend the entire day playing in the fields, collecting wild berries, and enjoying unadulterated fun and laughter. The days were long, and time seemed to stretch endlessly as we frolicked in the summer sun with pure childhood innocence.

The air smelt of fresh grass and cattle. Sheep, cows of various breeds, and horses dotted the fields, lazily grazing away. We had all the time in the world to sit and stand and stare at the beauty of nature that surrounded us. We hardly distinguished between the cattle grazing in the fields and our own band of carefree boys playing in the green grass.

Sometimes, even as a child the rebel within us would break the rules. I still remember the many times we stole apples from an orchard. We'd climb the wall at a less visible point, fill our pockets with stolen apples, and make our escape. We weren't always lucky—some of us would be caught, running with bulging pockets, apples spilling out.

Our family had now moved to Manchester and to earn money, we would scavenge for scraps of brass, copper, and aluminium—our equivalent of minted coins. We searched old buildings, garages, and sheds, favouring houses that were being pulled down after the war. The dismantled heaps often held a wealth of scrap. Each boy carried a bag, and when we had collected enough for the day, we would sell our haul to the local scrap dealer.

We knew a woman near a scrapyard in Manchester named Mary. After every scrap hunt, we'd take our findings to her, and she'd buy them from us. We never felt the need to give any money to our parents, nor was it expected. In Gypsy tradition, it was the man of the house who looked after everyone in the family until they got married or moved away.

With money in our pockets, we'd head straight to the fish and chip shop, eating to our hearts' content, and then if we still had money left, we would go to the cinema to watch the latest films. We loved watching movies together; the excitement of a new film would keep us talking for days—until the next one came along.

Once we ran out of money, we'd repeat the cycle, hunting for more scrap. In this way, we learnt how to earn money as boys—a skill that later became part of our livelihoods as adults.

Our escapades taught us survival skills early on. However, like every good story, my days of roaming, learning, and growing with my friends came to an end with the passing seasons. Our friendships seldom lasted more than a year because, as Gypsies, we moved constantly. Some families settled in one place longer than others, and over time, I drifted apart from my childhood friends. Like my boyish dreams, most of them faded, leaving only memories of the times we shared.

We cherished our freedom and learnt to survive and look out for one another, even as young boys. Those two vital lessons—freedom and survival instinct—were instilled in me early. I believe my childhood memories played a significant role in shaping who I became, helping me live responsibly as I travelled and raised my own family.

My parents came from a long line of Gypsy heritage, and we travelled a lot in caravans. Home to me as a child was always a caravan. It was never a house permanently built on land, and there was nothing unusual about living in a mobile home or static caravan. Sometimes, we would stay in settled accommodation, depending on the time of year. But mostly, we moved from one place to another, constantly roaming around the country without a permanent address.

Dad would go around farms collecting scraps from farmers, and we boys in the family would help him sort the different types of scrap, like cast iron, brass, copper, and steel. Often, he would take me along with him in his lorry as he did business with farmers who stripped old tractors, carts, and other machinery of anything valuable to sell to him. When he had collected enough scrap, he'd load it into his lorry and take it to the scrapyard to sell to the big scrap dealers.

Over time, Dad expanded into the lorry and caravan business. He would buy and sell lorries and static caravans, giving them a 'touch-up' that usually involved fixing or repairing engine and body parts and then repainting them. I still remember spending hours painting lorries by hand, as there was no spray painting in those days. It was backbreaking, manual work, but I never complained. Once the paint had dried, we'd take the newly transformed lorry to the auction to sell to prospective buyers. Every week, my dad went to the auction, and if he found a car or motor vehicle he liked, he would buy it and later sell it at a profit. When he had some downtime from his buying and selling ventures, he'd go hunting for rabbits, and we'd look forward to rabbit stew and other delicious rabbit dishes for dinner.

My mammy, on the other hand, ensured the smooth running of our family life. While the boys who were old enough worked with our dad, she took care of the household chores with the older girls. Our caravans and the compound where we lived were always bustling with children, and my mammy cared for everyone. She and the girls washed clothes and cooked daily, preparing delicious meals that brought us all together. Most of the cooking was done outside using cast iron pots over a firewood stove. My mammy made the best apple pie in the neighbourhood, and the aroma of a fresh pie wafting through the air was always a delight. The small gas stove inside the kitchen compartment was typically used for making tea and simpler dishes.

Since we had no running water, we used water stored in milk churns and barrels. Unless the weather was bitterly cold, we usually bathed with cold water. My mammy would wash the children one by one in a standard galvanised bath kept out in the open. The first child enjoyed clean, warm water, but by the time the last child got in, the water was cold and dirty.

My mum's favourite soap for washing us.

Lifebuoy was the bathing soap of choice, but it always caused the unpleasant problem of soap water running into our eyes and causing pain. The younger children, especially, would complain and even cry. My mammy would tell them to close their eyes tightly before applying the soap, which helped to some extent, though there was always a chance the soap water would still find its way into their eyes.

All types of washing, bathing, and most of the cooking were done outside. The caravans mainly served as our bedrooms, with one medium-sized room often sleeping half a dozen kids, depending on their age and size. Life always felt hectic in a large family, and there was hardly time to notice how fast we or the other children were growing and changing in stature and habits.

Today, when I'm asked if I would trade my upbringing as a Gypsy for another culture or a different lifestyle, my answer is always a resounding 'NO,' even though completing my school education would have benefited me a great deal.

CHAPTER 2

"Will You Marry Me?"

I remember it as if it were yesterday. It was afternoon, and I suddenly had a craving for a Mars bar.[2] The craving was so strong that I just had to go and get one. So off I went to the local garage shop.

As I entered, I could hear people shouting—someone wasn't happy. The noise was coming from the counter area, and I thought it would be wrong not to see what was happening. There was a young woman demanding her money back from the shopkeeper. She confronted him with such determination that he finally caved in and gave her the money.

On my way out, I ran into her and her friend and asked, "What was that about?" She replied, "The shopkeeper was trying to diddle me out of my change." I thought, this one's feisty, and I liked her style, so I asked if she and her friend wanted a lift home. When she said "Yes," I didn't realise it would be the first of many "yeses" for the rest of her life. I had found my future wife.

From the very beginning, I thought she was so beautiful. I immediately developed a liking for her and asked her out on a date. It took her some time to make up her mind. Finally, after what seemed a very long time of waiting, she agreed to go out with me. We went to watch a movie, but

---

[2] Mars, commonly known as Mars bar, was first manufactured in 1932 in Slough, England by Forrest Mars Sr. The bar consists of caramel and nougat coated with milk chocolate. Still available to this day.

I was so focused on her that I lost interest in what was playing on the screen. That day, on our very first date, while the movie actors played in reel life, I was enacting my romantic role in real life. As I turned my head towards her, I saw pictures dancing in her bright and lovely eyes. She had the most beautiful pair of eyes, and I wished I could drown in them and she would close her eyes forever. She turned to face me and spoke with her eyes, "What's going on?" I whispered gently but clearly into her ear, "Will you marry me?" She narrowed her eyes and replied immediately, "Are you mad?" I knew that she was completely taken by surprise, but I repeated, "Will you marry me?" She never answered my question, but six months later, we got married.

The traditional Gypsy wedding was out of the question for me and Patricia because, firstly, she didn't belong to the travelling community and, secondly, times had changed and my lifestyle had outgrown many traditional practices. In short, the traditional waiting period and other cultural aspects of marriage seemed outdated and quite boring to me. And more importantly, I couldn't wait to get married. Therefore, after confirming our love for each other and believing wholeheartedly that we were made for each other, we conveyed our sincere wish to our parents. When dad and mammy realised that I was serious about my decision, they met Patricia's parents, and after the preliminary meeting, they finally agreed on our marriage and set a date. The wedding invitation was sent by word of mouth to friends and family members of both the bride and groom. Soon, the entire Gypsy community and the locality where Patricia lived were abuzz with the news of our approaching wedding. Hectic arrangements and preparations were made, both at home and at the community centre where the wedding event was scheduled to take place. Patricia ordered a massive wedding cake, the likes of which I had never seen before. She also chose her own fabulous wedding dress, and when I saw the dress on her, she looked like a million dollars.

On the morning of our wedding, I was so excited as I rushed about to get washed and shaved that I cut myself while shaving with an old razor. I was appalled to see blood flowing from the blade wound, and for a moment, I looked into the mirror in horror and thought that I had messed up my whole face. Fortunately, the cut was not deep, and the bleeding stopped after a couple of minutes.

There were over 300 guests at the wedding, and they were all immaculately dressed for the occasion. All the women, especially those from the Gypsy community, were dolled up in beautiful costumes and dresses of many colours. But there was no comparison to the dress that the bride wore on that day. Patricia looked like an angel, so fabulous and stunningly beautiful. As I watched her walk down the aisle, I knew that I had made the perfect decision, and my joy knew no bounds.

Patricia and I were married that joyous summer day in 1966 in the esteemed presence of many well-wishers and distinguished guests from both sides of our families, who stood witness to our wedding vows and blessed our union and our future together. As we committed our lives to each other, my heart acknowledged that I wanted to walk the whole way with her "in sickness and in health, till death do us part." One of the elders wrote our names down in the large book, which would be there forever.

That day, we danced around the fire in carefree abandon with our guests and with each other. There was music and plenty to eat. We ate off slates, which are very popular in trendy restaurants these days—back then, we used them because they were easy to clean, and if one cracked, you just threw it away. For pudding, we had a variety of pies, baked apples, apple and raspberry cream, and custard, with cider to drink. The celebrations continued long after our guests had dispersed.

All in all, it was one big, happy wedding that brought great joy to the newlywed couple and much relief and happiness to their families and friends. It was a grand success because, no matter the culture, weddings are meant to bring families together and help the happy couple start their union off on the right foot—and our wedding did just that. I owe this to Daddy, who spared no effort or resources to make my wedding an event to remember for all time. His attitude was, "Patricia is giving my son something he has always wanted. So let me help my son get it." And Dad did just that by financing our wedding!

After our marriage, Patricia experienced cultural shock, and to this day, I wonder how she managed to cope with a new lifestyle and culture that was completely foreign to her. I still remember the day I first took her to the Farmer's Field with a 16 ft-long caravan. It had none of the modern amenities that caravans have today. Patricia was used to a life of comfort, having been raised in a proper home with an attached bathroom, toilet, and easy access to hot water.

On our very first day at the Field, she asked, "Where is the switch for the electricity?" and I handed her a match! Then she said, "Where is the water?" I passed her a bucket. As hilarious as it may sound, this was the kind of raw experience she learnt to adapt to over time, and I'm glad to say she did so beautifully.

Not many days after our wedding, my whole family—including my parents, siblings, and Patricia—would leave England and travel to Ireland for a holiday camp with our three caravans. It was emotionally difficult for Patricia, as she was bidding farewell to her family, friends, and the country where she was born and embarking on a new life as a newly married wife. But despite the cultural differences and the challenges of a new lifestyle, she somehow managed to cope and gradually adapted to her new environment and the people around her. She developed a close bond with my parents, who thought the world of her, and this healthy relationship greatly helped her, especially in her early years as a travelling woman.

Apart from being my devoted wife, Patricia became my helper, comforter, and encourager—and a year later, the mother of our first-born daughter, whom we named after her. Following the birth of our first child, my perspective on life changed dramatically. I seemed to have become a dad overnight, filled with excitement and a sense of achievement. The transition from being a son to becoming a dad and from being dependent on my parents to becoming self-sufficient and a provider for my family thrilled me. I embraced this new role wholeheartedly, committed to being a responsible dad. One year after our first child was born, Patricia gave birth to our first son, Michael. I was ecstatic with joy, feeling as if my status as a dad had been upgraded. My love and respect for Patricia grew even more, and I reaffirmed my commitment to being a loving husband and a devoted daddy.

In the years that followed, God blessed us with more children. Sisters Eileen and Barbara arrived as twins, and then we had triplets, though sadly, one of them did not survive. Only Thomas and Melissa made it through, completing our family of six children.

I worked hard to provide for my family. Like my daddy, I began my business collecting and selling scrap metal. It wasn't glamorous, but it provided enough to support us. I also started buying and selling lorries, cars, and caravans while running the scrap business during the day. I believed I was doing well as a businessman, daddy, and husband, but Patricia got disheartened somewhere along the way.

She seemed to grow tired and weary of the Gypsy lifestyle, becoming increasingly unhappy and started to express a desire to return to England. It became a routine for her to ask me every evening to sell our home. She also often told me she didn't want to die where we were settled and requested to be cremated. This went on for a long time. Each time, I would assure her I would do something about it, but in truth, I didn't take her words seriously. Occasionally, I would take her home to England, and we would travel by boat from Belfast to Liverpool. She would stay with her mother for a week, and then we'd return to our home in Newry. These trips would temporarily calm her, but after a few days, she would start asking me to sell the house again.

Then one day, while attending a church meeting outside of Newry with my wife and our children, a small American woman who was preaching pointed at Patricia from the pulpit and said, "Excuse me, sister, you in the pink cardigan. What is your name?" "Patricia Purcell." The preacher boldly declared, "The Lord says, He will tell you when to move." Then she turned to me and said, "Sir, you in the black suit, the Lord says, Take one step at a time." At that time, I had been asking myself, "Am I running where I should be walking?" and "Am I talking where I should be listening?" Patricia and I were stunned. Nobody but God and ourselves knew what we were going through. I saw the wisdom in the preacher's words. Patricia never asked me to sell the house again after that; she believed those words were meant for her and accepted our house as our home.

Since that meeting, the atmosphere in our home changed. There was a greater understanding and acceptance of life's realities, which helped us grow stronger as a couple and as parents. Our family life became healthier, and we felt content and happy.

When the days stretched long and peaceful and the nights were calm and quiet, I would sometimes tease Patricia and ask if I was mad to propose to her all those years ago. Even with six children, I would catch her by surprise and ask the same question. And, just like the first time, she would never answer. Yet her unspoken response was clear in the 55 joyful years we shared. To this day, I fondly remember those three little words— "ARE YOU MAD?" —escaping from her lips, and I know in my heart that I was not mad. Instead, it was the bravest and wisest question I ever asked: "WILL YOU MARRY ME?" Those four simple words laid the foundation for my life as a dad, granddad, and great-granddad.

***

Chapter 2 - "Will You Marry Me?" 33

Our earthly homes...

Patricia's first home with me

Our next home

The house Patricia would not move into.
It became our final earthly home.

Our home shortly after we moved in.
Yes, those are stone fish implanted on the drive.

Chapter 2 - "Will You Marry Me?" 35

A day with the family and friends

CHAPTER 3

Lost But Ignorant

During the Troubles,[3] we settled in the border town of Newry in County Down, Northern Ireland. My dad took over a car park on Edward Street and started a caravan business after obtaining a licence from the local authority. We sold mobile homes and rented out static caravans at an affordable and reasonable price. Our customers came from different communities, and we felt safe and happy because there was no shooting or bombing in that area. Almost everyone in town knew us, or at least knew our business well. We were known as kind and helpful people. Dad loved helping others regardless of their religious background and would even offer them loans to buy caravans. He would also lend me money so I could go on holiday with others in a caravan—but the catch was that I had to sell the caravan and bring the money back to him.

I travelled to different places, even across the border, to sell mobile homes and caravans. There was always an underhand transaction at the border with the customs officers. It was a regular practice and carried out without much hassle. The system worked to the benefit of both parties, but I would try every trick in the book to outwit the customs officers and get over the border while paying little or no duty.

---

[3] The Troubles in Northern Ireland, lasting from the late 1960s to 1998, was a period of intense sectarian conflict primarily between the Protestant Unionists, who identified as British and wanted Northern Ireland to remain part of the United Kingdom, and the Catholic Nationalists, who identified as Irish and sought reunification with the Republic of Ireland. Violence, including bombings, shootings, and civil unrest, resulted in over 3,500 deaths. The Troubles ended with the 1998 Good Friday Agreement.

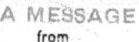

Front and back cover—proof of passing driving test

Inside pages

Chapter 3 - Lost But Ignorant

Driving Licence–Note: Registered to Edward Street Car Park, Newry

One day, I was taking a new caravan over the border. As usual, I was stopped at the border by the customs officers. I remained unfazed, thinking that they would allow me to pass after seeing my papers. But not so this time. They asked me to pull into the shed, and my papers were put in the basket. Having crossed the border many times, I knew what it meant to be asked to pull in. I could either be held up for a whole day and let go after making some payments, or simply pay a couple of hundred pounds and leave immediately. Neither of those options appealed to me, and I was left wondering what to do.

One of the customs officers informed me that they would be checking out the caravan and, depending on what they thought it would be worth, would determine the amount I would have to pay.

Whether it was my nature or just a good old sinner at that time, I was not paying.

I looked around and saw a cistern filled with water inside the caravan. An idea lit up in my mind, and I jumped into action. I started throwing the water from the cistern onto the ceiling of the caravan. Soon, the ceiling was dripping with water. When I was satisfied with the amount of water on the floor and the dripping from the ceiling, I called for the customs officer to come over. Opening the door to let him see, I pointed to the ceiling and said, "Who would want to buy a caravan with a leaking roof?" The officer looked up at the roof leaking with water and then at the wet floor. He looked at me, then back at the roof again. It was that look he gave me—that something was not adding up, but he didn't know what. He shook his head and said, "Off you go. You may leave."

Garda Checkpoint

Over the decades, I would have travelled across the border thousands of times to sell an equal number of mobile homes and caravans to an array of customers from different sections of society and communities, making profits by using every conceivable tactic and trick of the trade. Gradually, I expanded my business and started dealing with lorries and cars too. I would buy and sell different types of vehicles and make profits. I did well in business, and my life seemed to be going great, but deep in my heart, I always felt an emptiness, and sometimes I would feel a cry rising from the depths of my soul. However, instead of listening to the cries or paying attention to my feelings, I tried to suppress them with the help of alcohol or by indulging myself in worldly pleasures. To deal with my emptiness, I resorted to partying and nightclubbing. At first, it seemed to work, and I managed it well; at least that's what I thought in the initial years. But the feeling of emptiness kept coming more frequently, and the cries seemed to have grown louder and more urgent. My trips to the pub became more frequent, and I turned into a party animal. Soon, I was drinking my ignorant self to sleep without giving much thought to the state of my health or my family.

Unbeknownst to me, my habit was leading me to a fiery pit of hell, but I knew nothing better than to indulge in it. For decades, my life revolved around such a lifestyle, partying with people who would mostly fade away from my memory with time. Today, I can't remember having spent even a single day without indulging in drinking. If I knew anything that was fulfilling in life, then it was 'nightlife.' When night fell and most people were getting ready for bed, I would come fully alive, like a nocturnal creature who thrived on night activities, fuelled by a generous amount of alcohol. All the places that only a man without an iota of concern about his soul or his family would frequent—nightclubs, discos, house parties, you name it, I would be there. I tried almost everything that the world could ever offer to find a fulfilling life. I spent hundreds of thousands of pounds on nightlife. I was completely lost, but I was not aware of it.

The following story from my childhood days illustrates how I was lost but remained ignorant.

When I was a child, my parents would often take me along with them as they went around the streets to gather scrap metal and other kinds of stuff. We had a big, old lorry which dad drove around the neighbourhood to collect.

One particularly hot summer day, we pulled up outside of Manchester, where the street was lined with old, identical, red-brick houses. There seemed to be very little life around on that hot afternoon. After parking the lorry, Daddy turned to me and told me to stay put in the lorry while he and my mammy walked up the street, collected the scrap, and returned. He warned me not to get out of the lorry or I would be kidnapped or knocked down by a passing vehicle. I didn't realise, though, that he wanted me to sit there so nobody would steal the contents of the lorry or the lorry itself.

I sat in the cab of the lorry and watched them walk across the street, moving from one house to another. The sun was burning hot, and I was feeling very warm inside the cab. It didn't help to realise that even animals like cats and dogs had died in such heat. I was feeling weak, and my head was spinning as I saw a blurred image of my mammy about 15 houses away. I knew I had to get out of the cab, but at the same time, I didn't want to disobey dad, so I continued to stay inside until I couldn't take it anymore. I attempted to open the door, but I barely got it open. Back then, there were no electric doors or windows. After several attempts, I finally managed to get the door open, put my foot down on the running board, and onto the path. I looked around and saw a woman watching me from the front of her house. She appeared to have been watching me the whole time and said, "Excuse me, son. Do you want a glass of lemonade?" To me, that was the most pleasant thing to hear on that hot summer day, not only because of the heat but also because lemonade was my favourite drink. I happily said, "Yes," and she got me by the hand and took me into her house. She led me into the kitchen, sat me on a stool, and said, "Now, let me make you a nice glass of lemonade." I couldn't believe I was going to be served a big glass of lemonade. I sat on the chair and excitedly watched her prepare it. I can still remember the sound of the lemonade being poured into the glass… glug glug, glug glug. When she was finally done, she added a handful of ice to the glass and gave it to me. I thanked her, grabbed the glass from her hand, and took a mouthful of the drink. I carelessly swallowed a piece of ice and choked, but she immediately intervened and hit my back, and I was alright in a moment. As I enjoyed drinking my lemonade and playing with the items she gave me, I didn't realise I was lost and that my parents were looking for me. I didn't know how long I was in the house, and I had no idea that my parents had even informed the police and that everyone was searching for me, shouting, and calling out my name all across the street. I was playing with the toys and imitation money the woman had given me when I heard Daddy's voice. He banged on doors and asked if anybody had seen his child… his son. When he came to the door of the house I was in, I was petrified. It had never happened before, and fear gripped me as I thought Daddy would beat me. I couldn't find my voice, even though I heard him screaming out my name. As I opened the door, he saw me, grabbed me, and held me tight to his chest. I put my arms around him as he carried me back to the lorry and then back to the safety of our home.

This memory of my childhood reminds me of the many years I had remained lost without realising it. As a six-year-old child, that summer day, I didn't realise I was lost, and my daddy was frantically searching for me. And as a 40-year-old adult, I didn't realise I was lost, and my Heavenly Father was searching for me.

My body and my systems seemed to have adapted well to the lifestyle and trends of the time. My body was being fed and kept alive by all types of foods, including junk food and alcohol. My systems were well-attuned to the rhythm of nightlife. Life went on in this never-ending cycle of eating, drinking, and partying. I was in grave danger of losing my soul forever and ending up in hell. But nobody ever took a moment to tell me where I was headed or how I could be saved. I knew and dealt with a lot of people from my business around the coast. For decades, I bought and sold caravans to thousands of people, many of whom took my money, but that was it. There was nothing beyond business. I know today that they were born-again Christians among the multitudes who did business with me. They were saved and had found the way, the truth, and the life. They had once been lost but were now found. Yet, not once did any of them share with me about being saved in Christ. They didn't share the joy of finding their salvation with others. I hadn't realised what being born-again meant back in the 70s and 80s. I was just living my own life, a life of drinking and partying, which I considered normal. I didn't know that I was lost and dying spiritually day by day. The people who were born again and qualified to help me in my pitiable state of spiritual existence chose to keep silent. For reasons unbeknown to me, they never shared even a word of encouragement to help a lost brother find his way back to God.

Many years later, I met this same preacher at a meeting where I was sharing my testimony. He was shocked as I talked about how many Christians today have become greedy and keep Jesus Christ for themselves. They don't want to share their story of being born again or saved by the grace of God. They seem to be afraid to tell others about the saving power of Jesus Christ. I expounded on the need to share the truth if we have found it. The preacher and the congregation were blessed in that meeting because the words God gave me shook them and woke them up. They realised that, as Christians, they need to have a spring in their step and start telling people about Jesus before it is too late. They need to share the love of God—the same love that saved them from their sins—with those who are still lost. Sadly, for me, not one of them, not even the ones called to preach the Gospel, ever told me that Jesus loved me or warned me that my soul was in danger of going to hell. The Christians of the time, whom I met for business or social purposes and who had once been lost but were saved by the amazing grace of God, never mentioned Jesus to me. They kept the truth and the love of God to themselves, and I remained lost in my world of drinking and partying.

CHAPTER 4

We Have Our Religion

My journey to redemption and salvation began when a younger brother of mine, who had lived a life much like mine, called me after a long time to share his story of being born again. He had left his home in Northern Ireland to live in England. One day, out of curiosity, he attended a Christian meeting in a Gypsy camp. He realised that nearly every person in the camp was a born-again Christian. During the meeting, the pastor delivered his sermon based on John 3:3, *"Very truly I say unto you, no one will see the kingdom of God unless they are born again."* My brother interrupted him and said, "Oh, excuse me, we have our religion; we are Catholics."

The pastor turned towards him and said, "Brother, I am not talking about religion here. I am talking about Jesus, who died on the cross for every person on earth."

"I have never heard about this religion before," my ignorant brother replied, thinking it was a brand-new religion.

"Get a Bible, look up John chapter three, and you will see what Jesus tells you," the pastor replied.

That evening, my brother went to a bookshop to get a Bible. At the bookshop, he picked up different versions of the Bible and opened to John chapter three, where Jesus teaches a man called Nicodemus:

Now there was a Pharisee, a man named Nicodemus who was a member of the Jewish ruling council.

He came to Jesus at night and said, "Rabbi, we know that you are a teacher who has come from God. For no one could perform the signs you are doing if God were not with him."

Jesus replied, "Very truly I tell you, no one can see the kingdom of God unless they are born again."

"How can someone be born when they are old?" Nicodemus asked. "Surely they cannot enter a second time into their mother's womb to be born!"

Jesus answered, "Very truly I tell you, no one can enter the kingdom of God unless they are born of water and the Spirit.

Flesh gives birth to flesh, but the Spirit gives birth to spirit.

You should not be surprised at my saying, 'You must be born again.'

The wind blows wherever it pleases. You hear its sound, but you cannot tell where it comes from or where it is going. So, it is with everyone born of the Spirit." (John 3:1-8).

My brother was not convinced. He thought it was a new Bible published for a religion he didn't know, and he left the bookshop without making any purchase. The next day, he went to a car boot sale, where he met a woman who happened to be a sister in the Lord. He told her about the men in the camp and the pastor who had advised him to get a Bible and read what Jesus had said about the need to be born again to see the Kingdom of God. The woman put her hands up in the air and started thanking Jesus for bringing a lost soul to her.

She didn't sell Bibles herself, but she left her car and took my brother across the field to a sister who was selling Bibles along with other

Christian literature. There were Bibles in many different colours and versions, which he knew nothing about at the time. There were old, worn-out ones and brand-new ones. Thinking that the Bible he needed couldn't be one of the old, used ones, he ended up buying up to six old Bibles, wanting to be sure that among them he would have the right one. As soon as he reached home, he opened every one of them, and there it was. Jesus Christ Himself said, *"No one can see the kingdom of God unless they are born again."* (John 3:3).

'No one' means anybody who wants to see the kingdom of God must be born again. But as ignorant as he was, my brother wondered if the same scripture was in a Catholic Bible. So, he decided to go to a priest and ask him.

The good thing about chapels is that they are more open than closed; Protestant churches, on the other hand, are more closed than open. One would think that if you had a passion for Christ, you would be open more often than not. It was easy to find a chapel open, and in doing so, he found a priest and asked him, "Is John chapter three in the Catholic Bible?" Such a direct question caught the priest off guard to the point he was shocked and bemused.

The priest brought out a Bible, turned over the pages, and showed my brother where John chapter three was. He also took the time to explain that there's only one Bible, though it can come in different versions. Convinced that there is only one Bible and that it is the one true Word of God, my brother finally believed the words that Jesus says in John 3:3 and accepted Jesus as his Lord and personal Saviour. The scales were removed from his eyes, and he could now see clearly for the first time in his life. He realised how blindly he had been living in ignorance, unaware that his soul was on a dangerous path to hell. At that moment, he also became aware that the rest of the family's souls were in danger, and he couldn't wait to get to a phone to tell us.

It became apparent that the Holy Spirit, who had opened his heart and mind to make him see the state of his soul and save him, was now working through him to reach out to us. He was so excited to share his born-again experience with an earnest hope and a sincere prayer that we, too, would open our eyes and hearts to the truth and be saved.

You know one of those moments when there is something about a day unfolding in front of you, and you don't know what it is? This was that day!

There I was, all cleaned up, smelling nice, and dressed in designer clothes, ready to go out to a party, when the phone rang. Initially, it was one of those moments when you wish you hadn't taken the call.

I picked up the phone and answered, "Hello."

He excitedly said, "John, I'm a born-again Christian."

I didn't know whether to laugh or cry. I thought it was the stupidest thing I had ever heard in my life.

Immediately, I remembered my mammy's uncle, who claimed to have become a born-again Christian while serving a sentence in prison. He was known to be weird and always appeared somewhat out of the ordinary. I couldn't help but think that my brother had gone the same way.

I had enough problems; I didn't need any more. My brother was like a train on full throttle, unstoppable, as he excitedly shared his experience of being born again with me. I thought *Not another one who's become a gone-case and will end up with serious problems.*

"Get a Bible," he told me. "Yes, I'll get a Bible," I replied, but I had no intention whatsoever of bringing a Bible into my home. I was led by a religion and bound up in it, and I thought I knew what it was all about, without realising that I knew nothing at all.

Then I asked him, "Say, what is it like? Is it a letter from Jehovah's Witnesses or Mormons or what?"

"No," he replied. "This is the truth. Get a Bible and read it, and you will see what Jesus Christ tells you to do."

"Say, is it keeping you out of trouble?" I asked him, because I knew he was a wild man like myself. "Yes," he replied.

"Well, then I guess it's okay." I ended the conversation there and handed the phone over to my daughter, Eileen, indicating that she should talk to him. My mind was already in the pub, and I couldn't wait to get there. I let myself out the door and went to a party with my friends to feed my worldly desires. That night at the pub, I had a wonderful time drinking, dancing, and cracking jokes. I told my drinking buddies about my brother and his newfound religion, and we had a good laugh at his expense.

Following that day, my born-again brother started calling on the phone every night. Sometimes, he would call even at odd hours just to share his new experience with the Lord. It had become so bad that during one phone call, what had once been a pleasant chat had turned into something as irritating as a rottweiler barking at me. I began to think that all this talk was going to drive me crazy. No one wanted to answer his calls anymore. When I knew he was ringing, you would hear me shouting, "You get it! For goodness' sake, will you get it? Tell him I am not here. Say I'm out. I've gone away! Say anything, but don't put me on the phone." Whether it was religion or not, I didn't want to speak to him anymore.

CHAPTER 5

Homeward Bound

It was not many weeks after my brother got saved that my son Thomas and my daughter Melissa were going to their primary school. The headmaster, who was tidying up his office that day, saw them and called Thomas over. He said, "Thomas, I want you to take this Bible home and give it to your father." He explained that it must have been one of his uncles who had left it years ago in the school and forgotten about it. He handed the Bible to Thomas and said, "Off you go now; take it home to your father and remember to give it to him."

I realise today that God knew I had no intention of bringing His Word into my home. He knew my thoughts and the deficits of my mind, and He had His way of addressing the issue.

When I returned home from work that evening, Thomas came to me with an old-looking book in his small hand and said, "Daddy, the headmaster gave me this Bible."

"Did you ask for it?" I interrupted him, even before he could complete his sentence.

"No, Daddy. I didn't ask for it." Then he opened the Bible, pointed his forefinger to a page, and said, "Look, here's my uncle's name. The headmaster said so."

I looked at the still clearly visible handwritten name of my brother on the old Bible and realised that God had brought His Word, His Truth, into my home. He wanted me to possess it, read it, digest it, and live by it. He had chosen me. I did not choose Him. But what was I supposed to do with the Bible when I couldn't read or write? And what about my vices? How was I supposed to deal with my drinking and partying life? How was I to balance my worldly, sinful habits with the scriptures, even if I were given the ability to read in an overnight miracle? If someone had told me that day, "A few years from now, you'll be going around with a Bible, preaching the Word of God. You'll be in a hurry getting to meetings, busy saving souls." I would have laughed in their face and said, "It's pub time now."

And that would have been the whole truth of my life in those days. I was a husband to the pub and a father to the drink, and I didn't know it. I loved the pub. I had got myself so well adapted to nightlife that I had forgotten how to live in the light, literally. It had become an established norm for me to frequent pubs and parties almost daily. I was walking down the cold and dreary path to hell, but I could never figure out where I was going. But God had a different plan for me. And He brought His living Word into my life, which was dying in sin.

To many people, it comes as a surprise when I say that I cannot read or write. But that's the truth, and it still stays that way. Yes, I am illiterate. Nevertheless, God used my wife to help me learn and understand His Word. I'll go into more detail later, but to the credit of my wife, today I can quote many scriptures just from memory.

After being introduced to the Bible, I finally had something to tell my brother when he rang. But suddenly, for reasons known best to him and God, he stopped calling. He had been on the phone every night before I got the Bible, but it seemed like the moment I thought I had connected with the Word, I got disconnected from him. The calls stopped, leaving me wondering and wanting even more to share my

Bible experience with him. It was like putting a kettle on for a cup of tea when you're in a hurry—it seems to never boil, but it does. Then, about two weeks later, he rang again.

I took his call and excitedly said, "See, we got the Bible! My wife and I read it. And yes, we also read that scripture you told us about being born again. It seems alright. And you're not going to believe this: it's your Bible."

As expected, he was surprised and asked, "What do you mean, my Bible? I don't understand." I tried to help and said, "Do you remember years ago? The time you used to go to primary school. The headmaster is still there, and he says you must have left the Bible." "What would I be doing with a Bible in the school?" he asked, more to himself. "The headmaster found it, and it has your name written on it," I replied. "What?" he was truly surprised now. "I don't remember having any Bible in school, but well, if you say it has my name on it, then it must be mine."

Today, both of us realise that God had His special ways of introducing the Bible and His Son, Jesus Christ, into our lives. He knew us even before our birth and chose us to be the bearers of His Word and proclaim it to the multitudes.

God knows each one of us and everything about us. He is not deaf to our prayers or blind to our ways and habits. He knows our hearts' desires and our needs. He knew me and my brother even before we were conceived in our mammy's womb. And, glory to His name, He brought the light of His Word into our home to dispel the darkness we were living in and prepared us to reflect this light unto those travelling in the dark.

A few weeks went by, and my brother rang again. This time he said, "John, we are coming back to Ireland. There are some Gypsy families coming with us, and there are some pastors as well." He continued, "We are going to come into Cork with the caravans, and we are going to preach the gospel in different places. We plan to end up in Newry."

About a month later, they did come over. They preached the gospel around Dublin, Cork, and in other Gypsy camps. Finally, they arrived in Newry. But I had no space in my yard to host them because it was packed with animals and other stuff. Fortunately, another brother of mine, Joe, had a big yard with a massive barn in the middle of it. He allowed the caravans to pull in there. They cleaned out the barn and put up tents and seats. They made a makeshift stage, placing a pulpit in the centre and fitting the sound systems and musical instruments.

On the first night of the meeting, only my eldest son, Michael, from my family attended—and he was saved that same night. He returned home from the meeting and announced that he had committed his life to Jesus Christ. He always wore a crucifix around his neck, which I had bought for him, and I couldn't believe it when, right in front of me, he removed it, broke Jesus off the crucifix, and said, 'Jesus is not on the cross!' That really annoyed me; I thought it was surely sacrilegious. But then he continued, 'He arose from death and is with His Father God in Heaven.'"

My daughter, Eileen, went to the meeting the following night. When she returned home, she happily declared that she was born again. Both Michael and Eileen had repented of their sin and accepted the Lord Jesus Christ as their personal Saviour. They had been washed and cleansed by His redeeming blood. But… I laughed when my daughter came home that night and excitedly shared her new experience in Christ. I thought about what was happening to my family; it felt like we were under attack. But unbeknown to me, it was an attack of love, and God, who is love, was invading us. As it happened, I was next in line. I did feel happy for her in the depths of my heart, but at the same time, doubts arose in my curious and suspicious mind, and I decided to go over and see for myself what was going on in the meeting.

Chapter 5 - Homeward Bound

ABBA sang a song, "Money, Money, Money." We all had or have gods in our lives—those things that control us—and for me, it was money. It was my god before I was saved. Those gods are what we look up to and trust in.

I saw men walking around in suits and trendy clothes who wouldn't lift a pick or a shovel, men who wouldn't lift more than a pen. They walked about, greeting one another and attending the meeting with a mysterious smile.

So, I thought these meetings that my children were attending and getting caught up in this message of 'being saved' were just a new way of making a living. Whoever was running this business had a concept I wasn't aware of—a new way of making money and becoming rich. Deep in my crooked mind, I wanted to be like them; maybe I could get a piece of the action.

I got myself washed and presentable and went over to the meeting with one thing in mind: I would find fault or uncover the secret behind this so-called business of saving lives.

I entered the yard where the meeting was being held, and I couldn't believe what I heard or was seeing—you could have knocked me over with a feather. I'm not even sure if my mouth closed from the surprise.

The atmosphere was completely different—so friendly and inviting. I could hear beautiful music coming from the big barn where Joe had kept his horses. Walking into the barn, I suddenly found myself standing in a strange place.

For the first time in my life, I was attending a gospel meeting. I started to feel so awkward. My mind was telling me that everybody was watching me; I didn't know where to put my hands or where to turn my head. I had always been able to sort out problems and stay in control, but here I was, not knowing what to do. I said to myself with an underlying promise, "These cult people are not going to get me."

Somehow, I lost my hardness, the fighter, the haughty spirit, to the point I thought I had one last chance to escape. Slowly, and hoping no one would see me, I scanned the barn for openings, ready to run at any time.

One hundred percent of me was focused on finding fault, on exposing to my children the motive behind these people and how wrong they were… yet forgetting that here I was, sitting with a motive of my own, and it was just as wrong.

As the meeting commenced, it was as if someone had cemented my feet to the ground; I wasn't going anywhere, so I had no choice but to keep looking for what was driving their business.

I saw people with tears streaming down their faces—grown men and women. Why are they crying, I thought. Something awful must have happened in their lives. Or was the preacher wording his message in a certain way to draw empathy and then ask for more money for his services?

Wait to hear this! I literally couldn't believe it. In fact, as a gambling man, I would have lost all my money on this bet. My eyes caught a glimpse of people I knew from the pub and parties—men and women I used to drink and party with, real partygoers. They were now crying like babies, and my mind started to race, thinking, "There's seriously something not right here. Why aren't these people in the pub drinking and cracking jokes?"

I listened as the preacher delivered his message and listened intently to every word he spoke. I was disappointed that I couldn't find any fault. I found no mention of money being involved. If I had thought this was a new business, then I was right in a way, for it was indeed the Lord's business that they were carrying out.

"What did you do for My Son Jesus?"

At the end of the meeting, the pastor walked over to me as I stood by the door and gently said, "Do you know that God sent His Only Begotten Son to this earth to die for you?"

Shocked, unprepared, because it was the same words that had been written on a hayshed on the road from Bangor to Belfast. For years, each time I was on that road I would see those words, and over time I would learn what they said from a lorry helper, and now this man was saying the same words.

The hayshed on the road from Bangor to Belfast

I asked him, "What do you mean?"

He repeated, "God sent His Only Begotten Son to this earth to die on the Cross for you. And when you die," he continued, "your soul will go to God to be judged, and He is going to ask you, 'What did you do for my Son Jesus?' And what are you going to say?" He was beginning to rattle me; I could even feel my fists clenching and my breathing becoming heavier. For me, challenging me like this sounded cheeky. Plus, all this 'Jesus' stuff was all new to me, which was making me feel insecure because of the knowledge I had up to that point.

His question made me think about God and my relationship with Him, if it existed at all. I realised I was like a man who drives his car but never thinks about the spare wheel until a tyre gets punctured. Then there is a spare wheel alert: "Firstly, is it there, and secondly, can it be used and is it inflated?" But my choice is to either take it out and use it or sit and wait. For so many people, God is like that spare wheel. They never think about Him until something goes wrong in their life and there's a GOD ALERT! "Oh God, help me!" their voice shaking nervously. Is He hearing, or am I going to be struck down? Then, once the problem is fixed, we put Him away and forget about everything. That's how I had been using God all my life.

I couldn't give any answer to the pastor that evening, but each night I was drawn to go back to the meetings.

It was during one of those meetings that I heard about a massive Gypsy Christian Convention in France. I couldn't believe what I was hearing. Tens of thousands of Gypsies attended it every year, most of them with their families. The organisers would rent a large airfield, allowing several thousand caravans to park. An entire city would appear overnight for a week-long convention. Upon hearing this, I decided I needed to be at the next one.

Up to this point in my life, I had never been abroad or, for that matter, even taken a holiday down south—it was work, work, work.

With my wife being from England, that was a sort of a break for us when I would take her to see her family in Liverpool. Even then, I would leave her with her mother and go off drinking and nightclubbing. That was my idea of a holiday.

The meetings in the barn ended, and the brothers packed up and returned to England.

***

Much of my work involved transporting mobile homes, and some days I would be driving a couple of hundred miles all alone. When you're with yourself that amount of time, you do a lot of thinking.

One day, as I was driving alone, I started to think about the brothers at the meeting and the pastor. And the question for which I had no answer kept coming back into my mind: "What did you do for My Son Jesus?"

Suddenly, my body started shaking, and I didn't know what was happening. I became panicky. I thought that I was going to die or go mad and felt an urgent need to find somewhere to pull the lorry over as thoughts flooded my mind. "Is my life over? Am I going to die?" "Will I ever see my wife and children again?" "What about my brothers and sisters and friends? Will I see them again?" I needed to stop and stop now. Just then, I saw a layby ahead and pulled the lorry in.

I reached over to the key and switched off the engine. As soon as the engine stopped, tears started streaming down my face, and I cried like I had never cried before. Then, an overwhelming presence of something supernatural filled the cab of the lorry, and in that moment, no one had to tell me—I knew it was God. The atmosphere changed, and the presence of God was almost tangible. I had never felt anything like it, nor could I have explained it. Today, I know it was a divine appointment, an encounter that would mark me for life.

Even though I couldn't read or write, I always kept a little book with me for business purposes. I had adapted to drawing and using numbers to keep my records and run the business in a way only I knew best.

So, I took my book out and started drawing, listing all the good things that God had done for me in my life. He gave me a good wife, good children, good parents, good brothers and sisters. He gave me a good home and a successful business. He gave me my health, clothes on my back, and food on my table. He gave me the very air that I breathe.

I started filling page after page with my drawings, listing all the good things I could think of. Then I began another list, trying to record what I had done for Him. Nothing—can I repeat that—nothing came to mind. I couldn't draw anything in the book. I questioned myself, "Surely there must be something I have done for God?" But there was absolutely nothing I could think of. Once again, I was left without an answer.

With God's presence still upon me, I knew I needed Jesus Christ. There in that layby, I admitted my need for the Lord Jesus in my life. I closed my little book, switched the engine back on, and pulled out from the layby, driving home with a peace in my heart that I had never known before.

On the way home, I made up my mind to attend the Gypsy Convention in France.

Arriving back that evening to my wife and children, I told them that we were going on holiday. Immediately, they thought we were going to Liverpool. But when I told them we were going to France, their joy knew no bounds. Even our family dog started jumping happily on me, and I had to calm him down.

I called my brother in England to confirm the dates, and we only had a few days to pack up and leave for France.

CHAPTER 6

Loving Through Gritted Teeth

The year was 1992 when, for the first time in my life, I took my family to France to attend what is popularly known as *The Gypsy Evangelical Mission, Light and Life.*[4]

For a whole day, Patricia and the children (when they were available) got our large caravan prepared for the trip and stay in France. My job was to make sure our Land Rover was filled with fuel and the engine checked for the long journey.

I hitched the caravan onto the Land Rover, and the Purcell family was off to France. We took the boat from Ireland to England and then crossed the Channel to the French port city of Calais. We were all in good form. We were now a bunch of Christians trying to be a good Christian family, and everything was great—until we hit France… then hell was unleashed upon us. Not so much in a spiritual sense, but my ignorance took me to the brink of the doors of hell as my temper began to boil.

It was late in the evening when we got off the ferry, with only the streetlights illuminating the roads. There I was driving in France, as I would have driven in Ireland, on the left side of the road. It never crossed my mind that people would be driving on the opposite side to what we did in Ireland.

---

[4] The Gypsy Evangelical Mission in France (Life and Light) is a Pentecostal church active among Roma. By 2015, it would have 100,000 members and 260 churches.

We were approaching a roundabout, and I saw numerous cars coming around it the "wrong" way. I assumed the drivers were making mistakes. I drove around the roundabout the way I would have done back home, and to my shock, every car on it started blaring its horn. I said to Patricia, "Who are they blaring at?" She was as much in the dark as I was. Then she pointed out, "It's at you, John. Can you not see some are giving you rude signs?"

It was then that I realised they couldn't all be wrong. I knew then I was the one breaking the traffic rules and committing a grave mistake. When I got off that roundabout, I told Patricia I was not going another inch till morning. My new plan was to find a lorry to follow and hope they were going in the right direction. Patricia, being smart—very smart—didn't say anything. I so wanted her to say something, just something, to allow me to justify my actions. So, we stayed put for the night.

When I awoke, I thought maybe the worst was over, but how wrong I was. We had about 400 miles to drive inland. To help wake me up for the journey ahead, I got up early and took a brisk walk around the place. I started thinking about French cheese and grapes so vividly I could nearly taste them.

Off we went, with me in the driver's seat looking for grapes and my wife navigating using a large, clumsy paper road map. Do you remember those?

We were doing well staying behind lorries, as following them kept my driving sharp. However, this is hard to believe; after driving for many hours, we ended up right back at the same roundabout we started from. I was beyond frustrated. We were now going to be late, and it was Patricia's fault—she was the one guiding me. My whole body was trembling with anger, and voices were arguing inside my head: *"She was wrong for the past 400 miles; what makes her think she's right now?"*

Chapter 6 - Loving Through Gritted Teeth

I lost it. Four hundred miles of holding my mouth shut, and the floodgates burst. Everything spilt out of my mouth, and I was waiting for the kitchen sink to follow. I finished shouting when I had exhausted all my words. With nothing more to say, I looked over towards Patricia, and her seat was empty. *"Where did she go?"* I wondered. Scanning the area, I saw Patricia about 50 yards away, walking along the footpath. I wasn't even sure if I was still upset. Patricia had either not heard a word of my anger or God had spared her from it. I drove the Land Rover alongside her, trying not to shout, "Patricia, get in." She kept on walking. Embarrassed, I tried again, only a little louder, but still, everything seemed to come out wrong. "Get in, Patricia!" She stopped walking and looked at me in that way only a wife can. "I'm not getting in until you stop shouting." I said, "I'm not shouting!" in a loud voice. We men don't like to admit we're wrong. Guess what she did? She turned and walked off again.

Feeling desperate, I drove up alongside her again and said in a calmer tone, "Patricia, would you please get in?" If only she had just got in… but no. There had to be a condition. "Do not raise your voice to me!" Like a puppy with its tail between its legs, I said, "Okay, will you please get in?"

Back to square one, the Land Rover idling alongside my simmering anger. I waited for her to get into the cab and forced a smile through gritted teeth. "What way now?" I asked. She pointed towards a different road and, with a smirk, said, "That way."

I countered with a risky response, "I don't think so." But with no hesitation, she said, "Yes, it's that way." I mumbled under my breath, "Well, if you are sure. After all, you have the map." Back on the road again. It was the quietest road trip I had ever been on.

The plan was to end up in the middle of France where the convention was. And where did we end up with my wife's directions? She took us to Belgium. And that wasn't all. We went from Belgium to Luxembourg, then into Germany, and finally along the border of Germany and France. When we arrived in a city called Nancy, it felt like someone had put a kettle of anger on the stove again.

I was tired of mistakes, and in front of me now was a cul-de-sac. With a thirty-foot-long caravan behind my Land Rover, I refused to get caught out again. We can't have both of us making mistakes.

I pulled into the *cul-de-sac*, and we sat for some time at the side of the road, hoping someone would come along and confirm the right road to Paris. A few minutes later, I saw a woman walking down the road and asked, "Excuse me, do you speak English?" Whether it was my Gypsy Irish, or Northern Irish accent with a bit of English mixed in, she looked confused and went on her way. Then another woman came along with a child but couldn't help me either. What was supposed to be a holiday felt like hard labour in every sense.

Then I saw a man dressed in a suit approaching. I thought, *I bet he's been waiting his whole life for someone to ask him this question.* "Excuse me, sir. Do you speak English?" His face lit up. He looked into our vehicle and said, "Do I speak English? I speak English, German, Dutch, French…" and he went on, "Meet the son of a…." I had to interrupt him, "Please sir, I only want to know the route to Paris." He shook his head and said, "I'm sorry, but I am completely lost myself." Then he added, "And that is the truth."

He gave me some probable directions before walking away. As I put the engine in gear, I turned to my wife and said, "That's the stupidest thing I've ever heard in my life. A lost man trying to tell me the way."

Somehow, we did make it to Paris, and as we approached the venue for the convention, I couldn't believe what I saw. There were thousands of caravans and a sea of people spread across the airfield. I would learn later that 99% of the crowd were Gypsies. There was no drinking, fighting, or arguing. It was just a massive gathering of people mingling in good spirits in the name of God.

The Gypsy Evangelical Mission, Light and Life Convention

I looked around for the English-registered cars, hoping to find the brothers who had come to my brother's yard meeting in Newry, and finally, I found them—a whole group. There must have been around 50 caravans of English people, and I parked mine among theirs. Soon I was mingling with people I had never met before. They welcomed me into their midst with smiles and warm hugs, as if they had known me all my life. I could feel the love in their hugs. It was a hug of wanting to give something, not take from you. It was a hug of love and acceptance—a beautiful expression of the love of God.

After settling down to some extent in this new, friendly environment, I approached a brother and introduced myself to him. I expressed my sincere desire to be born again and asked him, "What do I have to do to be saved?" He was very pleased to hear that I genuinely wanted to be saved and counselled me. He introduced me to a couple of his friends, and together they took me into a caravan and prayed for me. From that day forward, my life completely changed. I accepted Jesus Christ as my Lord and Saviour. I thank God for the beautiful transformation that began that day in a foreign land.

I returned from the Christian Convention in France as a completely changed man. God helped me overcome my drinking and smoking habits. He snuffed out the cheating and lying nature from my life and began instilling His character into my new, born-again self. I started having a completely different outlook on life and people. God gave me His portion of love drawn from Heaven. It was a real love that could never be bought or compared with anything in the world. This love transformed me from a hopeless drinker, enslaved by sinful habits, into a man full of hope and faith.

I still remember those days when I would drive under the influence of alcohol, endangering not only my life but also the lives of others. I had become so accustomed to a life of drinking and nightclubbing that I would come home in the early hours of the morning, drunk. I would drive with one eye shut and the other focused on the white line in the road because with both eyes open, I would see three or four lines. That was the reckless way I lived—a life heading straight to hell. But I thank God for changing the direction of my life and giving me a new perspective.

Today, I take time to sit and observe my surroundings in the light of truth and understanding. I look at the creation—the mountains, trees, plants—that I never bothered to notice or think about before, and I marvel at the handiwork of God. I have shrubs and flowers around my home that I never knew were there or paid any attention to, but now I can see and appreciate them, and I view the world differently. Indeed, 'I was blind, but now I see.'

CHAPTER 7

Discovering Life with a Wife

Before we were saved, both Patricia and I lived by the standards of the world. There was no spiritual element to our lives—as individuals, as a married couple, or even as a family. It was saddening because we called ourselves Christians, yet we were living a life of lies and hypocrisy. We both came from Catholic backgrounds, and as a Gypsy by birth, I was raised attending chapel each week.

Even after our marriage, Patricia and I continued to attend chapel weekly, but we never practiced Christian values or principles. Our children grew up in an environment where Christ was not preached, and the need to be born again was never mentioned.

Led by us, their worldly parents, our children were blind and lost; together, we remained ignorant of the truth and the sad reality of our lives. Unlike a conventional Christian family, where parents lead and guide their children to salvation, it was my sons and daughters who first became born-again Christians.

They initiated and brought about a transforming change in our family. Following their example, I too was saved. It took a year for Patricia to see something different in us that made her want a taste of it as well. The good Lord blessed her, and she too was saved. God began to use her to help me become who and what I am today. Even before she was saved, she played her responsible role as my wife and as a mother to her children. She was like a mother hen who protected her family and took great care of all of us. After being saved, she became a vessel filled with the Holy Spirit and was used mightily by God in ways we could never have imagined.

Two of our children Eileen and Barbara

As I mentioned earlier, I am illiterate, and to this day I cannot read or write. But I can understand and quote scriptures today because of God's grace and my wife Patricia's relentless effort and sacrifice.

Deep in the night, while the world slept, we would stay awake as she read and taught me scripture passages, and I would try my best to learn and memorise the Word of God. Sometimes, she would read the same passage over and over, countless times, until I finally had it memorised. The routine would continue almost every night and sometimes for hours on end, but she never once complained. As dutiful a wife as she was, she seemed to understand that God had given her an added responsibility to read for me, and she played her anointed role without any complaint. It was physically draining and exhausting for both of us, especially when I was called to preach and had to prepare a sermon. There were times when I would repeat a single verse after her 100 times until I had it, word for word, in my heart and memory. The result of our effort was always worth every minute of preparation. We loved it, for we knew that we were deeply involved in promoting and expanding God's work. There was no greater satisfaction for us than seeing a soul saved, and over the years of our ministry, we have had the wonderful privilege of bringing multitudes of lost sheep back into the fold of God.

Patricia understood that my calling to preach the Gospel was a gift from God and supported me in every way she could. Yet, unbeknown to her, she was also gifted in a very special way, and it would take time for her to understand and accept her gift.

She had not been saved for long when she began hearing words in her head. These words would buzz around her mind without making any sense. It didn't hurt her, but it did annoy her, and she would try to block it out somehow. She would stop whatever she was doing, even if she was resting or taking a nap, and go downstairs to the kitchen. There, she would put the kettle on, make herself a cup of tea, and pretend as if she had not heard anything, or simply try to ignore it. But this strange experience continued, and she didn't know what to make of it until one day when she had another episode that left her deep in thought. As she sat alone in our bedroom, wondering what the words meant, she clearly heard a voice say, "Put it on paper."

Surprised but excited at the same time, she obeyed the voice. Closing her eyes, she wrote down the words floating in her head on a sheet of paper. When she thought she had written everything the voice had dictated and there were no more words left, she read aloud what she had written. She was pleasantly shocked. The words formed perfect sentences, and together, the sentences read as beautiful poetry that acknowledged and praised God!

One of her first inspired poems, titled *The Joy of Jesus,* reads as follows:

THE JOY OF JESUS

There's a joy in my heart, it is Jesus,
He made me his child, his own,
He gave me the gift of salvation,
He gave me the gift to write poems.
The words I write down are from Jesus,
To convey a message to you,
To tell you of the crucifixion,
How he died for you.
He suffered abuse and cruelty,
So he could save your souls,
It is only the blood of Jesus,
That can cleanse and make you whole.
So sit a while and think about what
Jesus did for you,
And when you understand, this is what you do.
Let him into your heart,
He will see you through.
Although we are not perfect beings,
Let's do the best we can,
Let's keep our eyes on Jesus
Instead of following man.

Chapter 7 - Discovering Life with a Wife

In the days to follow, Patricia would be led by the same voice to write other poems spread across different subjects but with one common spiritual element—Jesus Christ. In *The Old Woman*, she, as a poet, writes about a woman who gave her heart to God late in life after her husband had died and all her children were married. Throughout the lines, we can see and feel that Patricia could easily relate to the life and conditions, both past and present, of the woman in her poem.

THE OLD WOMAN

The old woman sits by the fireside,
Thinking of times gone by,
When she was young and first married,
When she first heard her baby's cry.
She pulls her shawl around her,
She remembers when she was cold,
Her frail old body shivers,
As she thinks of long ago.
They were poor, they hadn't much money,
But they had one another's love,
Her husband now dead, her children married,
She is left all alone.
She remembered the Christians preaching,
About the Word of God,
Would she go to Heaven or would her soul be lost.
She heard about the Christian meetings,
She wondered should she go,
Would she be on her own there?
Would there be anyone she would know?
I'll go, she said, and listen
It can't do any harm, to hear all about Jesus,
That night she gave her heart.

Some of her popular poems have been compiled into a small poetry book titled *POEMS—Messages from Jesus*, which is still available for purchase through John Purcell Ministry.

On the first page of her book, Patricia testifies:

> *"My name is Patricia Purcell*
> *I have been saved for ten years, praise God.*
> *When I was only two weeks saved*
> *God gave me the gift of writing poems.*
> *I have put together this book for the*
> *glory of God and to share His Word with you."*

Patricia remained steadfast in her faith until the end. The impact of her life and her contribution to God's Kingdom can be seen through her poetic works and, more significantly, in the lives of her children and her husband. The seed of the Word of God was able to take root in the soil of my heart and bear fruit because of Patricia's endless support and sacrifice. She trusted God enough to use an illiterate man like me to preach the Gospel to multitudes, even beyond borders and across nations.

On September 19, 2021, Patricia completed her mortal journey and went to be with the Lord. She was buried in Newry. Inscribed on her grave is one of her favourite poems:

THE TRAIN

> *The train pulls into the station Lord*
> *The people climb abroad,*
> *They come to face you, Jesus*
> *To ask, can they come.*
> *The Holy Book is opened*

Chapter 7 - Discovering Life with a Wife

They back away in fear,
You turn the pages, my Lord
Their names do not appear.
Their time on earth was wasted
They did not praise your name,
They were warned, Lord Jesus
But were not born again.
They closed their hearts to you my God
They also closed their ears,
Dear Lord, they did not want to know
They did not want to hear.
They had the chance to repent of their sins
But would not take a stand,
So listen now! If not born again
Your end will be dark and damned.

Until we meet again, my beloved

CHAPTER 8

The Day I Swapped Partners

We are a Gypsy family, and I praise God for the way He has blessed us mightily since we were saved. I have been saved for 32 years now and have never felt this happy in my life. Before knowing Jesus, I spent over 40 years bound up in a religion that, instead of guiding me toward God, seemed to encourage my worldly life of drinking and partying. I was also a womaniser, often telling fortunes in the pubs to draw a big circle of women around me. Looking back now, I see that I was partying my way to hell without even realising it. But I thank God for His hand of mercy that took me out of that darkness and brought me into His marvellous light.

Life was never the same after I decided to follow Jesus Christ. Every aspect of my life changed completely—personal, family, social, spiritual, etc.—and for the better. If someone had asked me what religion I was, I would have said, "Catholic," but I was more like a religious fanatic who didn't know anything about the God I claimed to serve.

Therefore, I wouldn't be far from the truth when I say, "I used to be a Catholic, but now I am a Christian." I was lost in religion from the day I was born. The reason for this is quite simple: Gypsy culture and the Catholic religion are entwined. Today, I know that religion, no matter what religion you have, cannot get you to Heaven. It is only

Jesus Christ who can get you to Heaven. What good is a building without its occupants? Likewise, what good is a religion without God? If you don't have God and the Word of God in your religion, then your religion is dead, and you are in deep danger of losing your precious soul too.

I remember going into a confession box. Crossing myself and sitting up straight seemed to make me feel more holy, and when the priest was ready, I confessed my sins. Thankfully, I know now that we must confess our sins only to God.

After I became a born-again Christian, the Bible was taught to me by the Holy Spirit the way it was written—not the way some man-made religion wants you to understand. I discovered that many rituals practised by churches today do not come directly from the Bible. We take great comfort in the traditions that have evolved over the years, and I'd say that's the same for many members of the travelling community. We also become comfortable with man-made religion that is detrimental to our spiritual life and the Church as the Body of Christ. In recent times, there has been a surge in people from these communities joining other Christian movements, with good reports and testimonies coming forth from various Mission Groups and Conventions. Many alcoholics, drug addicts, fortune tellers, and criminals are being saved in great numbers. They are not ashamed of their past anymore but are proudly displaying their new identity in Christ. Many of them have fully committed their lives and families to serving the Lord, moving from a worldly life to taking up a life of fervent Christianity as new creatures in Christ. *"Therefore, if any man be in Christ, he is a new creature: old things are passed away; behold, all things are become new."* (2 Corinthians 5:17). I am one among many who have been saved by grace from being lost forever. *"For it is by grace you have been saved, through faith- and this is not from yourselves, it is the gift of God- not by works, so that no one can boast."* (Ephesians 2:8-9).

Chapter 8 - The Day I Swapped Partners

Acknowledging that I was the vilest of sinners, saved only by God's grace, I dedicated my life to serving the Lord with all my heart, mind, and soul and asked Him to lead and guide me. From that moment I had swapped the devil for Jesus, and all I wanted to do was share the message of salvation, hope, and love with others who were still lost, like I once was. I wished to tell them the danger they were in of going to hell. My heart desired that they would know there is a God who can forgive their sins and save them from being lost forever. I longed and prayed to share what I had found in my Saviour, but I felt so inadequate and unqualified. One of the greatest obstacles was my inability to read or write. I had no idea how to refer to or cross-check the scriptures that were given to me as revelations. And most certainly, I didn't know how to gather or put to paper the inspirational thoughts that kept pouring into my mind. But God had a different plan: first, He chose my wife, Patricia, to become 'My Bible Reader' to solve my reading problem. Then He gave me the idea of drawing His revelations and interpretations in pictures to solve my writing problem.

It was a team effort, but I believe Patricia had to make more sacrifices because, even though we knew that we had been blessed by God in our new journey together and were being helped by the same Spirit, our callings were different. She had to be more patient, tolerant, understanding, and accommodating to my unusual method of learning and preparing my picture notes, many of which would become lessons that I would use as sermons while preaching as the days unfolded.

It was an exciting time for both of us as we began a new venture in pursuit of the Truth and joy in the Lord, settling into a local church in Newry as guided by God.

I knew that God was preparing me for something, but I didn't know what it was. I only felt this unspeakable joy in my heart as I made myself available to the promptings of the Holy Spirit. Patricia felt equally happy and supported me in every way possible, way above spending hours reading the Bible to me over and over again and organising my meetings, and would be my reminder of where I needed to be and when.

About four months after I was saved, a man approached me while I was attending a programme at the Newry Metropolitan Church. He asked me if I would like to speak at a meeting that was taking place in a month's time in Newry. I was pleasantly surprised and became excited. I readily accepted his invitation without asking or thinking much about it. After a month of waiting in earnest anticipation of sharing my testimony for the first time in public, the day finally arrived. I met the man at the venue, which happened to be a large hall that had previously been used as a bank but was now converted for events. We were happy to see each other and chatted together on the way into the hall; then suddenly I stopped mid-sentence.

We entered the hall where the meeting was to be held, and all I saw were white tables with chairs arranged around them, like those seen at weddings or business meetings. People were entering in droves, all dressed up, and soon the place was packed. I thought there must be other speakers lined up to speak. Suppressing my nervousness, my voice shook as I asked my host, "Where are the other speakers?" He turned to me and calmly replied, "You are the speaker, the only one." Dumbfounded beyond belief, the only thing that came out of my mouth was, "Where is the bathroom?" I felt I was going to be sick.

Somehow, I had pictured in my mind that it would be a casual meeting where I would speak in front of a few people seated most likely in rows, as in churches. But this was on a level far beyond the reach of my small mind. Inside, I was erupting like an earthquake; fear was having its dance with me. My mind went blank, wondering what I should share in front of these people whose faces appeared to say, "You need to be worth us coming to hear you."

When it was time for me to speak, my legs were like Elvis's, shaking all over, as I tried to look calm but was far from it inside. I thought there was no point in me opening a Bible, as I couldn't read it. Plus, I was only newly saved, and everything was all too unfamiliar to me.

Knowing I couldn't read the Bible, I shared the only thing I had in my mind: My Life Story. For more than half an hour, I stood there sharing my testimony of how I came to know Christ and surrendered my life to Him. I talked about my past life of drinking and nightclubbing and how I overcame such habits after becoming a born-again Christian. At the end of my life story, I urged my audience to accept Jesus Christ as their personal Saviour if they hadn't already, and I invited them to say the Salvation Prayer after me. It was my first time calling out and saying a prayer publicly on behalf of others, and I was amazed when three people gave their lives to Jesus.

After the meeting, I sat at a table to have some refreshments when a businessman from Newcastle approached me along with his brother. The businessman had been saved for 21 years, but his brother was not, and he believed his brother would be blessed to meet me and hear my story personally. I shared some pivotal moments of my life with them, stressing the time I was saved and how I gave up drinking and partying to live for Jesus. They thanked me for my time and left with my telephone number.

A few days later, I received a call from the businessman. He said that his brother was very impressed to hear my story and asked if I would kindly visit him and pray for him. I knew he wanted his brother to be saved too, and I agreed to visit. He thanked me, gave me the address, and informed his brother that I would call. When I arrived at the given address in Newcastle, his brother was eagerly looking out of the window, waiting for me. He greeted me warmly and led me into his home. As I followed him inside, I noticed he was shivering. He looked anxious, but he generally appeared a healthy person otherwise. We sat and chatted away for a long time, and then, prompted by the Spirit, I shared about the gift of salvation and invited him to accept the Gift and be saved. That day, in the presence of God and as witnessed by the Holy Spirit, he accepted Jesus as his personal Saviour, and my joy knew no bounds as I prayed for him.

Three years later, he passed away. Unbeknown to me, he had donated his body for medical research, so when I went to his funeral, there was no coffin. I thank God that he was saved. His acceptance of Jesus Christ as his personal Saviour, along with the three men from my first public appearance as a bearer of the message of salvation, made a powerful impact on my life and marked the beginning of my mission as a preacher.

I started to receive invitations from different churches, and soon I found myself busy travelling and sharing my testimony and the Gospel in various meetings across the counties. I relied completely on God for my lessons, and He helped me prepare them to use nature, childhood memories, life incidents, daily activities, surroundings, scenery, and even simple objects as inspirations. I would draw these on pieces of paper for easy reference and recollection. With no other means to prepare my notes or sermons, drawing became the only medium to record God-given revelations, visions, and inspirations.

CHAPTER 9

The Well Within

One day, when I was thinking about what I should preach at my forthcoming meeting, I was drawn to reflect deeply on a childhood incident that took place when I was nine years old. There was a man who had a well that had been passed down to his family. The well had been in use for many years. One day, he told my dad that he was building a new house and wouldn't need the well anymore because he was getting water piped into the house. He invited Dad to draw as much water as he could from the well. Dad thanked him, and the next morning, he hitched a trailer full of empty milk churns to his Land Rover, and we went to fetch water from the well.

When we reached the place and I saw the mouth of the well, which was the size of a car wheel, my mind began to wonder, "How are we going to fill all the cans from such a small well with so little water?" As Dad started to fill the cans one after another, I watched in amazement because the water in the well didn't run out. We filled all the cans and drove back home with our free water reserve.

As soon as I remembered this memory of the well, I felt inspired and moved by the Holy Spirit to prepare my sermon based on this revelation. I took a plain sheet of paper and started to draw the pictures forming in my mind using a pen and coloured pencils. With drawing as the only way and means by which to prepare my lesson, I began to sketch pictures from my memory, along with the revelations and scripture passages that followed. I know I wasn't gifted in drawing, as my illustrations in the attached pictures would show, but, like many such inspired moments in my past, I was happy when I finally finished my illustrative work. It felt like a masterpiece to me, and I knew it was priceless because God was going to use it to win souls. I thanked the Lord for His inspiration and carefully saved the picture sermon in my file.

When the day arrived for me to preach, I went to the meeting with my drawing and my Bible. But like in all my sermons, I wasn't going to use the Bible as other preachers would. Firstly, because I didn't know how to read, and secondly, because I was going to let the Word of God flow from my mouth as inspired by the Holy Spirit, using my drawing for reference and illustration.

That day, I preached on 'The Well Within Us and The Living Water.' It is a well of love, compassion, kindness, generosity, and every priceless attribute of our Lord. It is the well of the Living Water that never runs out and represents life, healing, the Holy Spirit, and the Kingdom of God. In essence, Jesus is the Living Water that provides the necessary spiritual nourishment for our souls to thrive. This Water quenches spiritual thirst and sustains and builds every believer in their walk of faith. The metaphor comes to life in John 7:38 when Jesus declares: *"Whoever believes in me, as Scripture has said, rivers of living water will flow from within them."*

But like the nine-year-old boy who didn't know that even a small well could contain so much water, many of us today don't know about the endless well within us. And yet, as believers, we are called to be the vessel from which streams of Living Water flow. This internal well, spring, or stream of water is also indicative of the Holy Spirit, who lives inside all who come to faith in Christ.

Chapter 9 - The Well Within

The Well Within message

In the New Testament, three references to water are given:

Jesus while speaking to the Samaritan woman, said in John 4:10, *"If you knew the gift of God and who it is that asks you for a drink, you would have asked Him and He would have given you living water."* Then in verse 13, He tells her, *"Everyone who drinks this water will be thirsty again, but whoever drinks the water I give him will never thirst. Indeed, the water I give him will become in him a spring of water welling up to eternal life."*

This spring of water is life in the Kingdom of God—which is eternal life.

Secondly, Jesus powerfully states in John 7:38 *"Let anyone who is thirsty come to me and drink. Whoever believes in me, as Scripture has said,* **rivers of living water** *will flow from within them."*

Here, Jesus was speaking of the Spirit, whom those who believed, trusted, and had faith in Him were to receive.

Finally, in Revelation 22:1-2, John writes *"Then the angel showed me the* **river of the water** *of life, as clear as crystal, flowing from the throne of God and the Lamb down the middle of the great street of the city. On each side of the river stood the tree of life, bearing twelve crops of fruit, yielding its fruit every month. And the leaves of the tree are for healing of the nations."*

CHAPTER 10

Boundaries are Defeated in Christ

As I continued to remain steadfast in my faith and my service to God and men, invitations began to arrive from abroad. The Gospel was taking me beyond my shores, and there was no holding back. I prayed and prepared myself in the great wisdom and plan of God, always remembering my past and keeping in mind that without Jesus I was, am, and will be nothing. But as Paul says in Philippians 4:13, *"I can do all things through Christ who strengthens me."*

My chance to preach abroad for the first time came when I received an invitation from a Methodist Church in Appleby. It was during The Appleby Horse Fair[5] in Cumbria, England. This event was held each year in early June, attracting around 10,000 Roma and Travellers, about 1,000 caravans, several hundred horse-drawn vehicles, and approximately 30,000 visitors. During the event, horses are washed in the River Eden and trotted up and down the 'flashing lane.' There is a market selling a variety of goods, including those traditional to the Romani and Irish Traveller communities, and a range of other horse-related products. The fair incorporates horse riding, horse trading, storytelling, and traditional music and dance performances, alongside the sale and display of traditional clothing, cuisine, and handmade crafts. Hand-painted Romanichal *vardos* and Irish Traveller wagons are also displayed at the fair.

---

[5] Previously known as Appleby New Fair.

The town was bustling with people and activities when I arrived, as I carefully made my way driving through the thousands who didn't believe in walking on footpaths. It was joyful to witness all the activity and excitement. There was no doubt that at one time I would have lost myself in the fun and enjoyment. But my focus was on my mission. I was looking forward to the meeting, hoping people might turn up.

Again, I was overwhelmed by the number of people who attended. The church was almost full when I took the stage. From where I stood behind the pulpit, I could see that people were still arriving in their own time. I started to share what was in my mind, but for some reason, I felt the urgency to preach about unity, peace, and love. And even though I didn't know exactly what references I needed to be using, I continued to speak as led by the power of the Holy Spirit. As I continued, I saw the minister of the church listening and smiling from where he was seated. I thought, *I wonder what is funny*. As I came to an end, I sent out an invite to the gathering to accept Jesus Christ and say the salvation prayer. That day, nine people came forward and gave their hearts to the Lord.

After I had said the prayer, the minister who had been smiling came to me and said, "John, that was directly from God!" He continued, "Last time, about a week ago, when I was preaching, a group of people didn't agree with my sermons and went on saying that we don't need to be saved; that all we need was to come to church. They tried to ruin the meeting. But today, when you came and preached, I couldn't believe what I was hearing. And I knew that it was straight from God, and that's the reason why those people listened to you and gave their lives to God."

I was surprised, greatly encouraged, and humbled by what he told me. We thanked God together for using us as His instruments of Truth and for His glory. We also praised Him for the people I was able to lead to the Lord on my first mission abroad.

My next opportunity to preach abroad came when I was invited by Evangelist Gypsy William Lee to preach at Easter in a tent meeting in Blackpool, England. When I arrived at the venue, I was met by William and his colleagues, who looked tired and helpless. When I asked him what had happened, he shook his head and told me to go around and see for myself. I drove down the lane to the area where the tent was supposed to be. The place looked like a freshly ploughed field. The large tent had been blown down to the ground because of a heavy shower, and I saw people walking over it. There were cars and caravans all around, and the whole place was a mess of muck.

Evangelist Gypsy William Lee with John

The people had started to leave when a group of policemen arrived. They wanted to know what was going on. I stepped out of my car and said, "I am a minister from Northern Ireland. All we are trying to do here is get the truth to the people." They asked, a bit confused, "What do you want?" I replied, "We need a place to hold our meeting." Then one of the officers said, "Follow us" and slowly drove away. As we followed, I noticed in the wing mirror that the rest of the vehicles were now behind us; we had a convoy of cars with a police escort. They led us into a football field, wished us all the best, and left. William and his team started to organise the event.

I focused on the topic of my sermon, "Imitation Love," using the deceitful nesting behaviour of the cuckoo bird as an example. However, I wasn't entirely sure if this was what the Lord wanted me to share. To seek confirmation, I began walking around the local housing estate, praying and asking the Lord for guidance.

Suddenly, I heard the most beautiful song I had ever heard in my life—it was a cuckoo singing, "Coo Coo, Coo Coo…" I was utterly flabbergasted. I looked around, but all I could see were houses; there wasn't a single tree in sight. Then I looked up and saw a cuckoo bird singing from a rooftop. My eyes welled up with tears, and my heart rejoiced at this clear confirmation from the Lord.

I spoke the following:

"The common cuckoo is known for its deceitful nesting behaviour. It lays eggs in the nests of other bird species, intending to fool the birds into rearing cuckoo chicks alongside their own. Being deceptive, it has no real love for its eggs or its chicks. The female cuckoo foregoes her parental duties and uses this deceptive method to propagate her species. Their eggs mimic the eggs of their host in colour and pattern to avoid rejection.

As I was sharing the above, I noticed some Easter eggs sitting on a table on the stage. I grabbed what appeared to be the largest one, hurled it to the ground, broke it into pieces, and said, "It is not about eggs or a piece of decoration. It is about Jesus!" The world seems to be filled with 'Mimicry Love,' imitation love like 'Mimicry Eggs.' Like cuckoos, we humans have become so deceptive, even when it comes to

Imitation love...

love. Like cuckoos, we don't seem to care anymore about our children and our families. And like cuckoos, we seem to show favouritism even with our mimicry love. There are hundreds of thousands of children today who do not know their real parents. They wish for and deserve to be cared for and loved too. They are being adopted and raised in foster homes. Those who don't make it to foster care end up on the streets. They are dying for want of care and love. And we can help them with the love of God in us. God's love is the only hope for our children, families, and humanity. It is not a mimicry or imitation love. It is the very love that prompted God to sacrifice His only Son, Jesus Christ, for us. The Bible says in John 3:16, *"For God so loved the world that he gave his one and only Son, that whoever believes in him shall not perish but have eternal life."* But we don't seem to understand this passage anymore; if we do, then we seem to have taken the love of God for granted. Regardless of our ignorance and sins, the invitation to 'believe and be saved' still stands today.

After delivering my sermon, I sent out an Altar Call, and 10 people responded. It was a great blessing and honour to lead them to our Lord that blessed day.

As the gathering dispersed, I noticed a man sitting behind a caravan who most probably didn't want to be seen.

I approached him and asked, "Are you alright?"

He replied, "I wanna get myself right with God."

I gently said, "Do you?" encouraging him to share his heart.

And he said, "I want to accept Jesus Christ as my personal Saviour."

Chapter 10 - Boundaries Defeated in Christ

On hearing these words, my heart leapt with joy, and after a brief interaction with him, I led him to the Lord in prayer. It was another miraculous experience for me, and I thanked and praised God for making His Spirit work in our midst to the saving of souls.

When I shared about this latest soul being saved with Evangelist William, he was noticeably excited and he asked me, "Which man? Which man?" When I pointed at the man behind the caravan, he took one look at him and exclaimed, "That man! That man is well-known by me, it can't be him, not with everything he has done. Surely, if God can save him, He can save anyone." We walked towards the man, and William shook his hand, and they hugged each other welcoming him into the kingdom. It was an emotional moment for the two men who had known each other for years. We took him inside his caravan and prayed for him, giving all glory and praise to God. That moment, like every moment in God, becomes etched in our memories.

After my mission, I returned to Newry in Northern Ireland and continued to preach Christ and share the message of hope and love. The memory of a fruitful trip in England was still fresh in my mind when I was invited by a man and his wife to preach at a house meeting in Armagh. I accepted the invitation and was looking forward to it. The meeting was conducted in the upper room of a big building and was attended by people of all ages. I shared about the Love of God and how it was different from worldly love, citing the common cuckoo as an example, as I had shared in the Blackpool meeting. I elaborated on fake, counterfeit, and imitation love, and on the loss of real love between men and women in today's world that leaves helpless children in foster care and on the streets for no fault of theirs.

After my sermon, unknown to me, there were six adopted children among the gathering at that meeting, and their adopted parents brought them to me so that I could pray for them. I was shocked, and so were all the people in attendance. One after another, they brought these children saying, "This child was adopted," "This boy has been adopted," and "This girl was adopted." It was an overwhelming experience to witness these children being introduced by their adopted parents. My sermon was being lived out by my audience right there, and I couldn't suppress my emotion as I prayed with a grateful heart for each and every child, thanking God for bringing them into a new and loving family.

With so much happening, I thought that would be all for the day, but I was in for another big surprise. The son of the man who owned the building told me that he was a born-again Christian, but his father was not. I felt his sincere desire for his father to be saved as he said those words, and I went to meet his father, who had already left the meeting and gone downstairs. I followed him to where he was and told him how his son loved him and how he must love his son too, and that was wonderful. But wouldn't it be even more wonderful if he were saved like his son. I gently hinted and invited him to accept Jesus Christ. That blessed day, the man accepted the Lord in front of his son, to the great rejoicing of angels.

After the meeting, I left Armagh with the memory of all the adopted children. On returning home, I pledged to remember them and pray for them throughout my walk of faith. I also thanked the Lord for giving me the right message to share with His people at the meeting and for being instrumental in leading another soul to His Kingdom.

In the years to follow, I would be invited three or four times to preach in the same place in Armagh, and every time I preached, it would turn out to be a great blessing not only for the congregation but for me as well.

The Philippines Mission

I committed myself to God in prayer, desiring only to do His will. As I prayed, I continually offered myself to God, expressing my willingness to go wherever He wanted to send me or to be used however He desired.

One day, as Patricia was sifting through my mail, a letter from a pastor in the Philippines caught her attention. It was another letter of invitation, sent on behalf of a local church in Bohol Islands, the tenth-largest island of the Philippines. At the bottom of the letter, there was a telephone number given along with the address. I decided to ring the number. The person who received my call had difficulties understanding my accent, and I had trouble understanding his.

After a while, he realised who he was speaking to and became extremely delighted. He said, "Hello brother John. We have been praying for you, your wife, and your children for a long time. When are you coming to visit us?" I replied, "I don't know." The next thing I heard was voices of excitement, as if he had heard me say that I was visiting soon. I didn't know what to say as he kept praising God and saying, "He is coming" to whoever was with him at the time.

Until that day, I had no idea where in the world the Philippines were. I ended up going to Easons bookshop and buying a world map. When I got home, I opened the map onto the table and had no clue where to even start looking. Then Patrica located it and said, "It's the other side of the world—literally." After finding where my invitation had come from, my heart sank. I thought it would be a crazy idea, a next-to-impossible mission for me to travel to an island.

But after making that call, I felt something had happened, even though I couldn't pinpoint exactly what it was. In the days that followed, I made further calls to the same number, and every time I called, I was overwhelmed by the joy and gratitude that poured forth from the pastor as he tried his best to understand and communicate with me. As for me, even though it was hard for me to make out his English, I could easily connect with his heart.

I took the idea that was forming in my mind to the Lord and it kept coming back; *"I would go anywhere for you Lord."* After many prayers and a few more calls, I decided to go to the Philippines. But was I ready, and did I have the resources?

After I had made my decision, I completely relied on God to provide me with the means and ways to travel. I knew that I wasn't going on a holiday but was carrying out a mission according to the command of God. Matthew 28:19-20 states, *"Therefore go and make disciples of all nations, baptizing them in the name of the Father and of the Son and of the Holy Spirit, and teaching them to obey everything I have commanded you. And surely, I am with you always, to the very end of the age."*

However, trusting God and having the faith that He was going to provide everything for the mission was not enough, even though I knew that it was His mission. I had to do my part, and I went about thinking what I could do, particularly for the finances involved. As I thought about it, my mind was directed to my yard. And when I saw all the things that had accumulated over the years without being used, an idea struck me. I was going to clear all the salvage out of my yard and make money from it. I would hold an auction!

I immediately called the Auction House, and they were all excited when they learned that I was selling my stuff. They used to do business with my dad, and they knew my address on the Dublin Road. They sent a group of people out to my house to have a look and sort through the items. They spent a few days taking out the things from the yard and sorting them one by one. Then they labelled each item with a number, and finally, we were ready. Among the numbered items were 40 ploughs, 3 steam engines, hand pumps, granite pillars, and troughs that had laid unused for a long time in my yard.

On the day of the auction, hundreds of people showed up, and the auctioneer was baffled to see so many people. Everything in the whole place that was up for auction was sold. I was amazed at how

Chapter 10 - Boundaries Defeated in Christ

John ministering in the Philippines

quickly all the items were taken. That day, there was a woman who was conspicuous in her manner and way of bidding, according to the auctioneer, who claimed to have seen her and said that she had stood in on everything that was up for sale. She would bid for an item, run up the price, then stop. When the auction was over, the auctioneer came to me and said, "John, was that woman your friend who ran up the price?" I was confused. "What woman?" He answered, "That woman who did bidding on every item and ran up the bidding but never bought anything." I was shocked because I had never seen any woman of his description. The auctioneer, who was equally, if not more shocked, revealed that it was because of the woman that all the items were sold at a much higher price than expected, and some people had also seen the same woman. On hearing this, I was dumbfounded. The woman seemed to have vanished into thin air. No one saw her after the auction. I took her to be an angel sent from Heaven to help me raise money for God's mission. Following this miraculous appearance and disappearance of the woman, the whole auction crew attended the church to hear me preach the following week, and the town was abuzz with the story of the angel in their midst.

The auction fetched £70,000, out of which £18,000 was deducted in commission. It was a large amount, and I was so grateful to God for it.

Soon, I was on my way to the Philippines with my wife and daughter, Melissa. It was a 24-hour flight that I will remember for a long time for a reason that was entirely separate from my mission.

We reached our destination safely after two layovers. At the airport, we were warmly greeted by a group of people waving at us. They took our luggage and escorted us to our hotel in small cars that carried only two or three people each. The weather was very hot upon our arrival, and my wife was struggling with the heat. Suddenly, the heavens opened, and it began to rain, bringing great relief. We thanked God, especially when we learned that the air-conditioning in our hotel room had stopped working.

While walking in the hallway, I noticed some creatures moving about freely—they were lizards that seemed to have escaped the notice of the hotel management. When I mentioned them to the receptionist, I was told it was actually a good thing to have these lizards, because if there are snakes around, they will eat the lizards. Seeing lizards is proof there are no snakes about, for now anyway.

That first night, we somehow managed to sleep, not because of the hotel's comfort, but simply because we were exhausted from the long flight.

The next day, we hired a jeep and headed towards the mountains, away from the city. As we travelled on, the roads gradually became narrower with uneven surfaces. We continued further into the jungle until we ran out of road. The road ended abruptly near the foot of a mountain, and we had to make the rest of the journey on foot. We cautiously followed our guide through the forest path and finally emerged at our designated village. I was completely drained and breathing heavily, but when I saw the happy faces of the villagers who were eagerly anticipating our arrival, I forgot the ordeal that we had just gone through and jumped back to life. We were greeted by the community elders and members of the local church, including schoolchildren.

We spent three weeks in the island nation, and during that period, I had the wonderful privilege of sharing the Word of God to thousands, or showing Christian movies like 'The Passion' in smaller gatherings, both religious and secular. It was amazing to see the impact of the Gospel in the hearts and minds of people from all age groups. They were so touched, even by the mention of the name of Jesus Christ, that many of them were moved to tears when I shared about His great love and sacrifice on the Cross for the sins of the world.

John ministering to students

In one of the meetings that was conducted in the auditorium of a big school, I was preaching about salvation to the staff and hundreds of students in their neat and tidy school uniforms. As I was preaching, I noticed a young man who was seated in the front row. He looked tough, stubborn, and seemed to be angry for no apparent reason. While others were focused on me and listening to what I was sharing, he appeared to be the least interested in what I was saying.

There was a skull, most probably a science exhibit, that seemed to have found a prominent place on a large table at the front of the hall. I took the skull in my hands and said, "This skull had a brain at one time. It used to be covered in flesh. It had eyes, ears, nose, mouth, etc., each with a separate nerve supply to constitute a head and a face. But now, it has become just a skeleton, a dry bone with no life in it. And one day, our head is also going to become like this skull. No matter how brainy we are, it will decay in death. Our mortal body is going to turn into a skeleton and finally return to dust. And it is given for all of us to die once, at our appointed time." The young man appeared to be listening now, and I continued, "We will all die one day and return to dust when our life is over, like the scripture says in Genesis 3:19: '...for dust you are and to dust you will return.' But our soul will live forever. So, it is very important to care for our souls too. Education, career, and jobs are all good, but it is better when we know where we are going in life and where our soul is headed. We must be very careful with our decisions and habits, lest our souls end up in hell for eternity. And the best time to make the right decisions in life is now, as young students who are the hope of the future. The choice you make today is going to break or make your future tomorrow. Make a decision to accept Jesus as your Saviour in your student life and live a blessed life of joy, love, and peace with an assurance of Heaven when you die."

I urged the staff and students to make decisions then and believe in Jesus so that they might be saved, and many of them gave their lives to Christ that day. When I invited them to say the Salvation Prayer, all of them joined in one accord and prayed, except the young man at the front. He neither accepted my invitation to be saved nor my call to pray. But after about 15 minutes, he approached me and said, "Sir, you make sense. I think what you say is right, and I want to make myself right." I knew that the Holy Spirit had touched him, and I prayed for him as he gave his life to God and got saved.

During the trip, I was able to preach the Gospel to various groups of people in different locations. Along with spreading the Word of God, I was led to contribute to alleviate poverty in the area we visited. I was particularly happy to contribute towards helping the children, most of whom were orphans and had been neglected by the local administration and the Government. When we went to visit the place where they lived, we found them together in a big makeshift hall. They appeared clean, washed, and dressed in their best clothes and even the building was spotless. The children looked excited and happy, but I could feel their hunger, pain, tears, confusion, and hopelessness behind their smiling faces. They were delighted to receive the cakes and buns we had brought for them. As I watched them relish their pastries, I wondered about their hopes and dreams and prayed in my heart that God would protect every one of them and guide them into their future. Long after I departed from these orphans and underprivileged children in the mountainous villages of the island country, I continued to pray for them and entrust their care and lives into the hands of the God who created them.

Overall, my evangelical mission to the Philippines was a blessed experience and a great success, made possible by grace and as commissioned by God. It was also one of the most memorable family trips that I had ever taken in my whole life. I still consider it a special trip that was fully sponsored by the Lord and was led and guided every step of the way by the Holy Spirit.

"Trust in the Lord with all your heart and lean not on your own understanding; in all your ways submit to him, and he will make your paths straight." (Proverbs. 3:5-6 NIV)

CHAPTER 11

Same Yesterday Today and Forever

There is a man and his wife I call 'A Miracle Couple.' They have a son whom I call 'A Miracle Boy.' About 16 years ago, they came to my house and requested me to pray for them that they might be blessed with a child. They were childless and had tried every possible way including fertility clinics, but to no avail. As a Christian couple, they sought the Lord for their child.

That day, I prayed for them with all my heart. I pleaded on their behalf to God, beseeching Him to bless the couple. I prayed for the wife that her womb might conceive.

Following our meeting and prayer, the wife became pregnant, and nine months later, she gave birth to the grandest little boy child that you saw who grew up to become 'A Miracle Boy.'

'Healing by faith,' as we read from the Bible, still applies in our lives today, and the following story illustrates how faith plays a crucial role in making miracles happen.

One day, while I was doing some household chores, I received a phone call from a young man who lived in Inverness, Scotland.

"Hello," I answered.

"Is this John Purcell?" the young man asked.

I said, yes, and he said, "You prayed for my mother 16 years ago. She had cancer, and the cancer left her body. Then you prayed for my uncle Jack, who was dying. We had called in that day at his hospital bedside to say 'goodbye' to him. You told me to put the phone to his ear and his organs would come alive. You started praying, and the organs started coming alive. The next day, he took a craving for a fish supper and after the doctors came round, he was sent home and never returned to the hospital again."

"I am ringing you today," he continued, "I have cancer in my liver. I am in a bad way, and I need your help. The Lord has led me to you that you may lay your hands on me."

"But you don't need to come from Scotland. I can pray for you now," I said, adding, "I recently prayed for a woman in America on the phone, and she was healed."

"No, no, no, I am coming," he was adamant, and he dropped the phone. I didn't know what was going on. Then he rang back and asked, "Where's the nearest airport?"

"Belfast," I replied.

"Right," he said and dropped the phone again. He rang back after a couple of minutes and said, "I have booked the seven o'clock flight that will be landing at Aldergrove Airport. Is that the nearest place?"

"Yeah, that is. I will pick you up at the airport," I said and hung up the phone.

Soon, I was on my way to the airport with a Christian friend in the Lord. We waited for our passengers to come out of the airport and greeted them. He was a young man in his 20s, pushing another man in a wheelchair.

After we exchanged our greetings, we all walked back to my car and as we got in, I sensed an overwhelming presence of the Holy Spirit. Suddenly, my friend started prophesying about the young man with cancer as if she had known everything about him from childhood. Then, prompted by the Holy Spirit, I began to speak about his drinking habit, his wife, and even about the kind of child that he used to be. It was a complete surprise for the young men, who had never experienced such a thing before in their lives. I laid my hands on the young man with cancer and prayed for his body to be completely healed in the name of Jesus Christ.

After the prayer, we said our 'goodbyes.' They thanked us and assured us they would keep in contact and finally left to catch their return flight to Scotland. When they reached home, the following day the young man with cancer made an appointment to see his doctor. At the doctor's surgery, they performed various investigations, including a CT scan, liver function tests, blood tests, etc., and are you ready to hear? The cancer was completely gone! His liver had started functioning properly, and the tests showed no anomaly in his systems. After receiving the test report from his doctor, he excitedly called me and informed me that he had been healed completely. I could not suppress my excitement as I thanked the Lord for His wondrous healing power and miraculous intervention that gave a new lease of life to this young man.

Following his testimony of miraculous healing and confirmation by his doctor, his whole family went back to church, and the young man never took a drop of alcohol again. He lives a healthy life today, free from cancer and alcohol. Since his miraculous healing, he has shared his testimony in many meetings organised mainly by the Light and Life Missions in recent times. His name is Joe Townsley, and his testimony, which is available even on YouTube, is a great inspiration for the multitudes who delight in the miraculous works of God and rest their hope in Him. It also teaches others how to pay heed to the voice of God and follow His instructions to see miracles happen.

When Joe and his family learned that I was publishing my story, his brother Sandy, who was with him at the time of his healing inside my car, happily agreed to write his side of the story, which greatly surprised me because right now, as I am confirming what has been written, for the first time I am hearing Sandy's account, which is inspiring to me. It would only be right to let him tell you his story in his words. Enjoy.

> *Hello, my name is Sandy Townsley, and this is what the Lord has done for me.*
>
> *I was born and brought up in a Christian family. I am the youngest child in my family.*
>
> *Both my parents and all my siblings were Christians. I was raised in church from about four years old. We lived in Perth, Scotland, and attended church regularly.*
>
> *One day, our church held a tent meeting. It was there that we first saw John Purcell. I was very young and can't really remember it well, but at the meeting, my mother and father got John's phone number and kept it ever since. For years, my family walked with the Lord, and we held house meetings where local people would come over. I remember my father, mother, and brother Joe having fellowship, and I remember Joe reading his Bible. That was the environment I grew up in.*

We moved to Aberdeen and continued to attend church for years, but I never really listened. I didn't understand God or religion. Eventually, we drifted away and even stopped going to church. Years passed, and now I was in my late teenage years. None of us were walking with the Lord, and that's how it stayed for a time. The only person who still went to church was my mother. In 2016, my mother was diagnosed with cancer. She had to go for an operation, and she phoned John Purcell before her operation and asked him to pray for her, that it would all go well and bring healing. John prayed for my mother, and everything did go well. She was miraculously healed, and she's still fine today.

Just a few short months after that, my uncle was taken to the hospital. I can't even begin to write all the things that were wrong with him. He had so many problems: his kidneys were shutting down, his oxygen was dangerously low, and his lungs were in a bad way. He was at the end. My father got a phone call from the hospital, and they told him that if there was any family who wanted to come in, they should come because he was going to pass away at any time. My father called John Purcell and asked him to pray for his brother, who we thought wasn't going to make it through the night. John had a time of prayer with my father, and thank the Lord, the very next day, my uncle recovered and was eating fish and chips. A miracle that only God can do. My uncle is still okay now, and it's 2024.

But even after that, none of us walked with the Lord. A couple of years later, I met my wife, and we moved in together. Then all my family moved down to Fife, and for five years of my life, I drank every single night. I would usually leave only one day in a week to be sober. During those drinking times, it would be 10-15 beers a night, and then it went to 20 beers, and when that wasn't enough, sometimes 30 or 40 bottles of beer every night.

Within two years, I put on 12 stone in weight. I ended up at 34st 10lb. Also, I ended up unnaturally depressed to the point where I literally didn't want to speak to anyone. I used to hide the fact that I was depressed because I never wanted people to think I was having such mental problems. I suffered from extreme panic attacks. Sometimes I would sneak away from my wife and sit crying in secret. I believed in my mind that at any moment I could die, and that was the way I lived those five years—a prisoner of my mind. The only person I could talk to was my brother Joe because he lived almost the same life. The only difference was that he had been drinking for 11 years, and he had 6 children, and he hid the drink from them so well. My brother Joe and I are unnaturally close. He's my brother and best friend. We would sit for hours together and wonder how on earth we were like this, how we could have such an amazing family, and still not be happy in our hearts.

As years passed by, I kept putting on weight so much that I couldn't even lie down anymore. I could only fall asleep sitting up. I ended up developing a problem with my heart called Supraventricular Tachycardia (SVT). Sometimes, my heart would instantly jump to 200-250 bpm (beats per minute) at the slightest sudden movement. It came to a stage where I became too depressed and scared to move in case I had an SVT attack. I was at the lowest point in my life, and I can't even put into words how deeply affected I was mentally. Yet, all I could think about was alcohol.

Then in 2023, a friend of mine that I hadn't heard from in months called me up and told me that he had given his life to Jesus. I was thinking in my head at the time, I really can't be bothered listening to him. I was at church for years, but I only heard about Him; I never knew God personally. Anyway, this friend kept calling for a couple of weeks. He went on about how he met with Jesus, and he kept telling me about this TV show called The Chosen. *It was a show about Christ. He kept going on and on about it, telling me to watch it. So, I did. I watched the first episode and was not interested. But it wasn't until the fourth episode, where Jesus was standing in Simon's boat and asked him to cast out the net. Jesus performed the miracle where the net was full of fish and breaking. Then Simon dropped down in front of Jesus and said, "Depart from me, for I am a sinful man." It was then and there, like a lightning bolt, the Lord revealed Himself to me for the first time, and I had literally just cracked open a beer when it happened. I instantly knew Jesus was the true Messiah, the Lord of the universe, the Creator of all things, and that I was a sinner. Just like Simon said to Jesus, "Depart from me, for I am a sinful man," I felt the same, but I did not want Jesus to depart from me at all. And then I fell on my knees and cried out to the Lord. That day, I accepted Jesus Christ as my Saviour and surrendered my life to God.*

I knew that I was saved, but I was still an alcoholic, weighing 35 stone, and I didn't know what to do. I was overwhelmed with joy, to the point where I had 101 different questions and didn't know where to go. So, after a few days, I went to my brother, Joe, who was saved years ago. At the time, he wasn't walking with the Lord, but I knew he had studied the Bible years ago. I went to him and started asking questions about the Bible and such, but what I didn't know was that the Lord was working in his life as well. However, at the start, we couldn't talk about Christ, the Bible, or anything like that to our families, as we were far too embarrassed.

So, for a while, it was only me and Joe talking about God and His Word. I would drive over to his place, and we would go for a ride so we would be by ourselves. Then we would have a wee Bible study or a prayer inside the car so that our wives wouldn't see us. Even when I was at home, I would ask my wife not to come into the other room lest she saw me reading the Bible, and that's how it went for a short while. Not long after, Joe gave his life back to Christ and I couldn't have been happier for him.

One day, my parents were at my house and my mother's phone rang. I could overhear easily because her phone was loud, and you could hear almost everything. It was my brother Joe, and he said, "Mummy, I was at the doctor's, and I have cancer." And there and then, for the first time in my life, the Lord spoke into my heart instantly, and all He said was, "Don't be afraid. Your brother is going to be healed." Normally, when anything is wrong with my family, I'm always the first one to panic, but not this time. I can't put it into words, but all I can say is there wasn't even an iota of fear in me. It was like the Lord had removed it, and even if I wanted to be scared, He would not allow it.

As soon as He spoke to me, I stood up, walked to the hallway, picked up my keys, jumped in the car along with my wife, and drove over to Joe's place, who lived about six miles from me. I prayed the whole way, asking the Lord what it meant and wondering how my brother could have cancer and be healed. I didn't understand what He wanted me to do, and I kept praying for Joe, asking the Lord to give him peace of mind and let everything be okay. When we got to my brother's place, I realised that my mother and father had followed me over as well. My brother was sitting out in his driveway in his van. Immediately, we all started speaking about what was going on. I felt it weird talking about hospitals and appointments, etc. In my head, I couldn't care about any of that because I knew and believed in what the Lord had told me ten minutes ago, and the Lord not only told me but also gave me peace with it.

But it wasn't until my brother said these words that I had to open my mouth and say what the Lord had told me. Joe said, "I've drunk for 11 years straight. I've squandered my life. My youngest is five years old and I'm going to be dead and gone, and she's going to grow up and not even remember me," and a couple of other things. I told him, "Joe, I don't care if the doctors have said you only have two days left to live. You are going to be healed." That's how confident I was; I knew what the Lord said was true.

The very next day, I remembered this man, John Purcell—his name just popped into my head. So, I called my father to ask for John's number, but as soon as he learned why I was calling, he said, "Sandy, your mother was just on the phone with John. She has requested him for prayer." I spoke for some time and hung up. As soon as I hung up the phone, I got a message from Joe that read, "Sandy, I am thinking about looking for John Purcell." I texted back, saying that I was up for it and told him that father had his number. Joe got the number from my father, called John, and arranged to fly over to meet him in Northern Ireland that very day. My brother knew that it was from the Lord that he had to go to John and that he would pray for him. He believed that the Lord would heal him then.

So that very day, we got the flight tickets and flew to Ireland after telling John about our arrival. During the flight, we talked and wondered what this man would be like and why the Lord wanted us to meet a stranger we had only seen once as little children. About an hour later, we landed, and as we were walking out of the airport, John was standing, waiting for us. Within the first 30 seconds of meeting John, I knew he was different from anyone I'd ever met before. There was this gentleness and aura about him that cannot be described. He asked us to jump into his car. There was a lady in the front with him, and me and Joe slid into the back of his car. John explained to us that he was going to pray for us, and he believed the Lord was going to heal Joe. He said that he was nobody special and that it wasn't him but the Lord who was going to do the healing, and then he started to pray.

As he was praying, he began to say, "The Lord has put it in my heart that the reason you have cancer in the liver is through alcohol." I remember thinking to myself, "How can this be? How can he know if it wasn't for the Lord revealing it to him?" He continued to pray, and this is where I can honestly say that never in my life before had I ever felt anything like it. Sitting in the car with John praying, both me and my brother felt the presence of Jesus with us in the back of the car. The same Jesus who performed mighty miracles was sitting in the back of a car with me and my brother, removing cancer from his body. I could sit from now until next year trying to put into words the absolute power and sheer unbelievable, unimaginable presence of Jesus Christ that blessed day. The only words I can use to explain how it felt are: We were like newborn babies, and Jesus picked us up in His hands and comforted us. I knew instantly that the cancer was gone from my brother's body.

I thought back to the time when the Lord said to me, "Don't be afraid. Your brother will be healed." I also remembered what He said to my brother about his need to go to Ireland and meet John Purcell, who would pray for him, and he would be healed. And the Lord has fulfilled it. But I can say with certainty that my brother's healing wasn't the only reason why we were meeting John Purcell that night. As much as we didn't know John or the woman who was with him, they also didn't know us. We were complete strangers to them, yet they turned to us and said that the Lord had revealed to them that we were suffering from depression and that it was also going. We prayed again for that and for other problems that it was impossible for them to know. They even told me in detail about certain things that I'd told no one. Then John told us that we must strive for the Lord every day and not to look back.

It was time for me and my brother to get out of the car and part ways, and as soon as I opened the door of the car and my foot hit the tarmac, for the second time that day, the Lord spoke to me: "Now is your time, go back and be a light to your family and the world forever." I will never forget these words until the day I depart from this earth and meet the Lord. Most amazingly, He also said that exact thing to my brother Joe at the same time, and we could recite each other's words. Suddenly, everything seemed to fall into place, and I realised then and there that the whole reason why we had to come to John wasn't just for my brother's healing. That was just the bonus; the main reason was that God wanted to heal our whole family and bring us back to His fold, using our worst nightmare to be the biggest miracle we'd ever seen in our lives.

John came out of the car and hugged us. He gave us some CDs, and we parted ways. From that night of meeting John Purcell, I have not touched alcohol and have remained sober since. Where I once used to drink at night, the Lord has replaced it with fellowship with other brothers in the Lord. I've lost 5 stone, and where I once used a wheelchair to move about, I can now walk around freely. My depression left me that very night, and I still can't believe it's gone. I've been to many Christian mission fields, able to walk and attend tent meetings and meet with brothers and sisters in the Lord. Unlike my lonely past, I have so many friends today. But most importantly, we, as a family, listen to the Lord now and try our best to be a light to one another and to those travelling in the darkness of a sinful world.

Today, every person in my family at the age of understanding has given their life or come back to Christ and is active in church life. This year, my brother Joe shared his testimony with nearly 6,000 people, and I thank God for granting him the opportunity to glorify His mighty name. After sharing his testimony, as Joe left the stage, a lady came up to him and said, "I know the man you met in Ireland. It was my father." John's daughter was in the tent that day, and it was a true blessing and an amazing experience that could only have been made possible by God.

In my life's journey, I have been to many places and met different people, but I have never come across anyone like John Purcell. I know and understand that John is only a man, and he can't do anything on his own. I know that it's only Christ who can do anything, but I thank God for John's faith that allows God to work miracles through him. I am so grateful and blessed that in this age, we have a true apostle like John Purcell. I thank and praise God that this man, who was a stranger to me, was used by the Lord to not only heal my brother from cancer and restore him but to heal and save my family. Through John, the Lord opened Himself to my family again and revealed His miraculous works and plans for us. I agree that some of my family members were already saved, but God used John to be that final push we needed to bring my entire family to His Kingdom, and through us, many others in a ripple effect.

Today, I acknowledge with all my heart that God's timing is perfect. Through divine purpose, we were unbelievably reconnected after 20 years to this gypsy preacher in God's perfect timing. It was at a tent meeting in Perth, Scotland when we first saw John in 2003, and two decades later, in the winter of 2023, through divine connection, we met him in the back of his car at an airport in Northern Ireland. And life was never the same again.

John's love is encompassing, and his faith is supernatural. It could only be a gift from God to have such faith as he has. He is a modern-day hero to me, and I pray that one day I will also have the gift of faith like him. My experience with John, along with my brother Joe, is one among thousands of others in which John has been instrumental in performing the wondrous works of God, and I have personally met many of them who have been saved, miraculously healed, or blessed in different ways. I thank God for John and wish him good health, love, joy, and peace.

Sandy, October 2024.

How can we say *we are born again* and not believe in the God of miracles? Surely, being born again is a miracle in itself. The Bible clearly says in Hebrews 13:8, *"Jesus Christ is the same yesterday, today, and forever."* He continues to perform miracles all over the world, and He is the only One who can do it. If we are open as a willing vessel for Him, then He can fill us and use us for His glorious purpose, including healing. I give all praise and glory to His name for using this vessel of mine according to His will and mighty purpose. He has charted the course of my life's journey, and by His grace and wonderful purpose, I have travelled to Holland, the Philippines, New Mexico, England, America, and the Republic of Ireland—to many different places to preach Christ and bring about salvation in the lives of many souls.

Some people ask me, "How can you run a successful business? You just drop everything and go away for weeks." But ever since I was saved, I have learnt how to put God first and always listen to His voice and follow His instructions. Sometimes, that means abruptly halting my business and being sent away to places and people of His choosing. God is my first love. The Scripture tells us in 1 John 4;19, *"We love because He first loved us."* It is the effectual love of God that first changes our hearts and makes us capable of love, and it is His example of love that reminds us again and again of our need to love other people. When we love God, we can love every person on this earth, not just one group of people. And I thank God that He has given me this love for everyone, no matter what nationality or race they are, and no matter what religion they practise. He has given me love, particularly for the lost souls. A loving God that He is, He has shown me never to look at any man with prejudiced eyes. We must not love a person based on their wealth or property, or how important they appear to be in society. We must look at their souls and preach the Good News in the strength of God's love and wisdom, so that they may be saved from being condemned to hell.

It is given for the saved to seek and save the lost. We are chosen to be soldiers in the army of God, and the battle is not won in the trenches. We need to get out into the battlefields and fight with all our might. We need to come out of our comfort zones and start telling people about Jesus Christ in all boldness because they need to know that hell and eternity is real. We must remember that we are living in the end times. There are multitudes lost to the world today, and the love of our Lord within our hearts should compel us to seek them with the message of hope and love.

The times we are in call for every soldier in God's army to bear their full armour and keep fighting the good fight. It is crucial for us to regain our lost ground by winning the souls of those struggling with drugs, alcohol, immorality, and other soul-damning habits, so that they too may be saved and say with joy, "I was blind and lost, but now I see, for I am found."

CHAPTER 12

Caged or Not He is Worthy of Praise

Daddy died 42 years[6] ago of cancer and Mammy died three year later.[7] We, the siblings, gradually separated to live our own lives. I continued to live in Newry but in a different location. I have a fairly big place on the main Dublin Road that in the past became a home not only to my family but also to a lot of friends from the animal kingdom. My interest and love of animals began in my boyhood days. As a young boy, I grew up loving and playing with cats and dogs. My dad even kept sheep and pigs as pets. We also had horses that were used to pull the caravans. As kids, it was always great fun to watch a horse with the caravan trying to negotiate steep hills and sharp bends. A horse pulling a caravan uphill on a rainy day would always attract a crowd of excited children and even the old folks.

I also had an uncle who dealt with animals on a large scale. He used to rear cattle, sheep, and horses and sell them off to buyers from different places and countries. He would export horses to Belgium, sheep to Dublin, and cattle to other European countries. It was no surprise that I became fond of my animal friends from an early age. As I grew up, I became more attached to animals and began to keep other pets aside from the common cats or dogs. By the time I was happily settled as a married man with children, I had acquired a variety of animal species that inhabited my land and co-existed with me and my family. At one time,

---

[6] Although we have used the word 'years' throughout the book for consistency, these two instances have been written as John would say it—'year.'

[7] See note 6 above.

my private collection included llamas, alpacas, donkeys, ponies, a massive two-humped camel, and a pot-bellied pig, among other small creatures. I even planned to add two tigers to my collection and made all the arrangements by contacting the concerned authority, but when I realised how dangerous and unpredictable tigers were, I threw away my plan at the eleventh hour.

Of all the animals, my favourite was the two-humped camel which I bought from an Italian circus. I christened her 'Camilla,' and despite me being charged with 'murder of a camel' she became one of my prized possessions. I'll tell you about her later.

My love of animals continued, and their numbers kept increasing with the addition of new species. Every time I added another animal to my collection, I would tell my wife that I had bought it for the children, and she would tell me that I was the biggest jackass of the lot. But to be honest, I wanted the animals for myself and was using the children to obtain my desires and, in the days to follow, to fulfil my interests in God. My mini zoo was located by the side of the busy Dublin Road, and it used to attract many curious visitors. Various travellers from all over the country would stop for a while from their journey to take a tour of my property.

And just like many incredible ways of God, He started using my animals for His purpose. For many years, God brought people from every walk of life to me using my animals, and I have had the wonderful opportunity to lead many of them to the Lord. One day, a curious visitor who had come to look at the animals asked me, "Why have you got so much stuff around your home?" and I simply replied, "Well, we are fishers of men, and we need all the bait we can get to draw them in." I praise God today for leading thousands of men and women to His fold through my testimony and my property.

The Lord has done mighty things in my life that are beyond human understanding. He has used this once-broken vessel of mine to perform miracles of saving lives, healings, and many wonders. I have seen cancer patients made completely whole, and I have been a witness to the healing of every type of illness and disorder through the power of our Lord Jesus Christ.

***

The Lord has given me love for every person on this earth. Therefore, the love that I have today is not for one group of people but for all the people that He died for. The Lord has also given me a love for animals, and as mentioned at the beginning of my story, I keep a lot of different types of animals, and they have become a part of my extended family in God.

Each week I would go to town to buy feed from an animal shop for our animals. The shop owner had hamsters, goldfish, pet rabbits, cats, puppies, and all different types of animals. In the middle of the shop, there was a large cage with a parrot in it, and every time I walked into this shop, I would ignore the people around, pass through all the animals, and go straight to the parrot and sing, "My shackles are gone. My spirit is free. Oh, praise the Lord. He lifted me." It became a routine for me, and I continued to sing to the caged bird every time I went to buy animal feed. The shop owner, who had watched me singing to his parrot for nearly six months, called me over one day while I was there and said, "Mr. Purcell, can I have a word with you?" I said, "Sure. What is it?" He took a heavy breath and began, "I have noticed you for the last six months. And every time you come to my shop, you go straight to the parrot and sing to him, 'My shackles are gone. My spirit is free… la la…'" He continued, "I want to explain something to you. That parrot has been with us for ten years now and has not spoken one word." Then, with a friendly voice, he concluded, "So what you are doing is only a waste of time." I nodded my head in response and left the shop with my purchase.

I did the same thing the following week. I went to the shop, walked through the building, went straight to the parrot, and sang, "My shackles are gone. My spirit is free. Oh, praise the Lord. He lifted me." As I was leaving the shop after buying my stuff, I saw out of the corner of my eye the shop owner shaking his head, as if to say, "This man is gone."

A few days later, I was sitting in the living room of my house and looking out from the window. As I was idly looking out, I saw a car coming in at about 40-50 miles an hour. It passed by the side of the house and I could recognise the driver—it was the shop owner! I thought he had come to kill me or someone. He seemed to be in a great hurry and abandoned his car in haste. Then he ran to my door shouting, "Mr. Purcell! Mr. Purcell! Mr. ...!"

I was walking over to the door and shouted back, "What is it?"

"Quick," he said excitedly, "The parrot... the parrot is singing. The parrot is singing your song, 'My shackles are gone...'"

It was my turn to get excited. I never opened a door so quickly; I thought I had taken the hinges off. I ran past the shop owner, who was still trying to explain it all to me, jumped into his car without even thinking of bringing mine, and shouted at him, "Com' on, hurry up!" We sped out of my drive and into Newry as if the cops were after us.

When we reached his shop, there were a number of people gathered around the cage, and the parrot, to my greatest amazement, was singing, "My shackles are gone. My spirit is free. Oh, praise the Lord. He lifted me." Not a word missing, singing perfectly—better than me, even—and those who stood around had joined in the singing.

It was quite an experience, especially for the shop owner and those who knew about the parrot's inability to speak. I was amazed, and to this day, I attribute the miracle to the wonder-working power of our

Lord Jesus Christ, by whose name the blind can see, the deaf can hear, the dumb can speak, and—am I allowed to say it?—the parrot sang!

John's sketch of the caged parrot that sang "My shackles are gone."

I couldn't wait to share the story with my family and friends. However, at the same time, I was reminded of the deception of human nature. I knew most of the people who were gathered there that day; one of them was waiting on a medical report; another man had a serious financial problem; a couple of them had marriage problems, and there was yet another man with a heavy drinking problem.

I could see all of them, with their burdens, singing excitedly, "My shackles are gone. My spirit is free. Oh, praise the Lord. He lifted me." I could understand their excitement in the moment, but deep down, I could feel and understand the state of their souls behind their smiling faces. It's like when you ask a person, "How are you doing?" The usual response is, "Oh, I'm doing great," with a smile.

Then, as they enter their own little world, they pull the curtains, sit in a dark room, or lie on the bed, with their pillow wet with tears. Can I just be direct? You might be saying one thing, but your heart is saying another. Somehow, you are entangled with fear and hurt, shackled to your burdens.

God wants you to surrender all your burdens to Him. He wants you to be free. I can tell you from my life in God: He can move mountains, no matter how big they are. Yes, no matter how massive your problems seem—be it a marriage problem, financial crisis, health issue, or any other burden—I don't care what label is on it, because I know with one hundred percent certainty that Jesus Christ can move it. He can solve all our problems, no matter how impossible they may appear. If we pray with faith, believing that He is going to move that mountain, then He will move it. I have seen mountains of problems that satan had put in front of me moved by God. Many times, I tried to get over a mountain by my own strength, but every time, I fell back down. Lying there at the bottom, helpless and alone, I didn't know what to do because I hadn't been born again yet; I hadn't repented for my sins unto Jesus, and I wasn't saved.

But today, having already repented for my sinful past unto my Saviour, Jesus, and having been washed and cleansed in His blood, I have become a child of God. My Father in Heaven hears my prayers and answers every one of them. If you are praying with faith as small as a mustard seed, God will assuredly answer your prayers. He will move what is in front of you and clear the way—this I know. He is faithful to Himself, and He always keeps His promise.

CHAPTER 13

Kissing the Pig

One day, I was driving from Newtownards to Bangor when I remembered a man who lived on a large plot of land somewhere in between. I had heard about his interest in animals, including the wild ones he kept on his property. He would attract visitors, especially school children, who came to see his animals. He was known for rearing them and selling them off to prospective buyers. Being an animal lover myself, I had always wanted to add a deer to my private animal collection. So, I pulled my lorry into his place and asked if he had any deer for sale. Unfortunately for me, he replied 'No.' Not wanting to leave empty-handed, I enquired if he had any other animals he was looking to sell. He said, "Yes," and showed me a large pot-bellied pig in a pigsty.

"How much do you want for it?" I asked.

"Two hundred and fifty pounds," he replied.

"One hundred and fifty," I countered.

He said, "Two hundred," to which I agreed and paid him.

The man bound the pig's legs and carried it around the corner of his building, but then he suddenly stopped and asked, "How are you taking this pig with you?" I said, "In the lorry." He replied, "But where? It's a flatbed lorry!" I suggested putting it in the cabin. He looked at me as if thinking something was definitely not right.

We managed to lift the pig into the lorry cab, and he tied it with a rope to the cab seat. With a bit of oinking, the pig seemed to settle. I said goodbye to the seller, and off we went, the pig and me, heading towards home. I wish I could tell you that was the end of the story, but it wasn't.

Within a few minutes of hitting the road, the pig went berserk. I nearly thought it was demon-possessed. It went so crazy that the rope broke free from the chair, and—dare I say this—it started to relieve itself, spraying everywhere; the floor, the door, the seat, and all over me. It had no preference as to who or what was being covered.

The smell was choking me, and I could only put my window down a little because the pig suddenly had the idea to get under my legs and attack the steering wheel. Between trying to fend it off and drive at the same time on a dual carriageway, I gripped the steering wheel with both hands, as if I were strangling it, afraid the pig's snot might somehow seep through and cause the lorry to veer off the road.

You have to remember this was during the Troubles, a time when army checkpoints could pop up temporarily on the roads to stop and search vehicles for wanted terrorists, guns, or explosives.

As the pig and I rounded a corner, I thought, "Not today, no, not today." But there it was; several vehicles in a queue. And why, you may ask? The army had set up a road checkpoint, and inevitably the pig and I were going to get searched. Stuck in the queue and waiting for the army to search selected vehicles, I knew we were going to be there for a while. I looked at the pig and shook my head.

Chapter 13 - Kissing the Pig

As we approached the checkpoint, a young soldier held up his hand, signalling me to stop. He approached my lorry cautiously, eyes sharp, clearly wary in case it was a trap. The closer he got, the more I started to sweat, and suddenly I found myself shouting, "Don't open the door! Don't open the door!" But that didn't deter him. He climbed up the steps of the lorry, and as he peered through the window, I thought he was going to be sick. His face twisted in horror, and he immediately turned away. Between the sight and the smell, he jumped back down and waved me on, shouting, "Go ahead, you. Go ahead!"

I drove away thinking, this pig is costing me more than money. The lorry cab was like a slurry pit including me, oh I could not wait to get her home.

When we entered my yard at home, I was so disgusted with the pig and the state of the cab I chucked the pig out and shouted, "I never want to see you again!"

But believe it or not, my worker Tommy, developed a fondness for the pig and named her Miss Piggy. Over time, this fondness blossomed into a deep friendship. Tommy spent hours with Miss Piggy, and she seemed to understand him perfectly, responding to his commands and even sharing his meals. They were inseparable. However, just when everything seemed to be going well, Miss Piggy fell ill.

I noticed her lying down in the pigpen one day when she would normally have been trotting about after Tommy. She looked lethargic, completely drained of energy. Her eyes seemed dull, and she refused to get up, even when I tried to coax her. She was cold to the touch and breathing heavily. I knew she needed help immediately. The only thing that came to my mind was the CPR[8] training I had taken years ago.

---

[8] Cardiopulmonary Resuscitation (CPR) combines rescue breathing (mouth-to-mouth) and chest compressions to temporarily pump enough blood to the brain until specialised treatment is available.

I called Tommy, and together we carried Miss Piggy into the garage, where it was warmer. We put on the heat and laid her on a makeshift bed. I began massaging her body to keep her blood circulating and give her some warmth. Tommy stood there, watching helplessly, and asked, "What are you doing?"

"I know what I'm doing," I replied. "I can do CPR."

Then he said, "Tell me what I need to do."

I looked at Miss Piggy and then at him and said, "Hold her mouth, Tommy. Hold her mouth."

Tommy held Miss Piggy's mouth and asked, "Now what?"

"Kiss her Tommy. Kiss her… She's dying. Quick, quick. She's dying," I urged him.

He lingered over Miss Piggy then shouted, "No!" "You'll make me a laughingstock in town and you'll tell everyone I kissed a pig."

Tommy refused to kiss Miss Piggy, and there, right in front of our eyes, she breathed her last.

I shared this story about Miss Piggy in one of my sermons at a certain hall, adding that Miss Piggy wanted her best friend—the one she trusted completely—to kiss and save her. But when she needed him most, as she lay dying, her wish was denied. Her trusted friend could have kissed her and may have brought her back to life. He could have saved her, but he let her go. That's the way the story goes, though, of course, Tommy's kiss wouldn't have made any difference in the life or death of Miss Piggy.

However, the matter of truth is that, in this world, many people are

Chapter 13 - Kissing the Pig

John's sketch for his Miss Piggy message

dying for want of love or attention from friends, family, and other loved ones. But the people who could easily afford to give or share their love often shy away from giving away what was so freely given to them by God, who is Love. They deprive others of love and compassion, leaving them miserable and broken-hearted. Yet, to love and be loved is the greatest gift of life, and in sharing our love, we only allow it to multiply and grow. In loving, both parties—the one who loves and the one who is loved—greatly benefit and contribute towards a happy and healthy relationship. Our world would be a better place, and life would be much easier and happier if we could all master the art of loving our fellow beings without reservation or prejudice.

When I delivered my sermon using Miss Piggy's story as an example, I was met with blank stares from the congregation. There was no hint of understanding or appreciation of what I was sharing. I felt so disappointed and wanted to end my talk abruptly and disappear from the pulpit. My audience seemed to have turned themselves into statues, and I felt like a fool. I somehow managed to conclude my sermon without stopping midway and in a decent way. After the service, I returned home feeling so discouraged and began to think that my preaching days were over. But the next day, I received a call from a woman who would change my perception of preaching and show me God's wondrous ways.

The woman asked, "Is this John Purcell?"

I answered, "Yes."

And she said, "Hello, John. I am calling to thank you."

I was surprised. "But why? And how do you know me?"

She replied, "You preached in our hall last night. My boyfriend and I were there, and both of us got saved." I listened to her, all amazed, as she continued, "After hearing your sermon, we decided to give our lives to God and remain committed to each other forever."

I was so excited. "Thank God! Thank God! God bless you."

After we had said our goodbyes and exchanged blessings, I began to realise how wrong I had been in my way of thinking. I sought forgiveness from God and promised Him that I would never again judge others based on what I see or feel. Instead, I would humbly do my part by concentrating on my role as a minister who has been called to preach Christ and salvation. I would play my role to the best of my gifted ability and leave the rest to the Lord.

Since that day, I have remained committed and reaffirmed in my faith, and God has always been faithful to perform His mighty works through me.

CHAPTER 14

Discovering the Gift

Before I was saved, I used to joke an awful lot about hell. I even made jokes about nightlife down in hell with women, drugs, and drinks. There were times when I felt that hell-based jokes got much more laughter from the crowd than the usual pub jokes, and I seemed to be quite innovative in coming up with new ideas and jokes about hell. The truth was, I knew of hell, but I did not really know anything about it. My unforgettable experience with a camel in the following story would reflect my knowledge and understanding of hell.

For reasons known only to God, I have always wanted a pet camel, for as long as I can remember. Even as a child, I would imagine camels in the desert and be fascinated by the thought. I had seen the film 'Lawrence of Arabia" many times, it was one of my favourite films. Each time I saw it I would say to myself, 'I'll have a camel of my own one day.'

Over time my desire for a camel had dropped to the back of my mind; but aren't you glad that God's promises never do? The Bible says, *"He (God) will give you the desires of your heart,"* (Psalm 37:4). The key, however, is in the beginning of the verse: *"Take delight in the LORD and He will give you the desires of your heart."* I hadn't realised it, but as I was simply in love with Jesus, I was, in fact, taking delight in the

Lord according to Scripture. In doing so, I experienced the fulfilment of a desire I had long forgotten. As I share how my long-awaited desire came about, keep in mind the desire you have and delight yourself in the Lord.

John with Camilla and son

I was coming back from Dublin, driving my lorry, and in those days, one would pass through Dundalk town. As I was driving through, I saw the biggest circus that I had ever witnessed in my whole life. The troupe was from Italy and had come with hundreds of animals including… a whole load of camels. I was particularly excited about seeing the camels, and I said aloud, "I want one!" as I drove away. I kept thinking of camels and how to get one all the way home, and when I finally reached home, I told my son Thomas that I might have seen the biggest circus in the world. I told him about the different types of animals I had seen and expressed my desire to buy a camel. He did not reply to me, but I was too excited to listen even if he had said something.

That night, I went to bed early, but could not sleep. I was like a child, excited and more excited. I stayed awake thinking about the camel and wondered if the circus people would sell me one. I was joyous at the prospect of owning a camel from my childhood dreams and riding it.

When the next day arrived, I drove to the circus, taking Thomas along with me in a brand-new car. The circus was not open when we arrived. We drove around and met some people and talked to them, but none of them seemed to understand English. I heard them speak what I believed was Italian. As they spoke, they kept pointing towards a big wagon in the circus ground, and I thought, "The boss must be there." I went and knocked on the door of the wagon, and out came a young man who happened to be the circus manager. He was Italian but spoke English. After exchanging 'hello's', I told him the purpose of my visit.

I said, "See, I keep a lot of animals myself, but I don't have a camel, and I have always wanted one." I continued, "I wonder if you have a camel for sale." He looked at me up and down as if to say, "Are you real?" He didn't speak for about two minutes, and I was getting uncomfortable to the point of being embarrassed and thinking, "What is he going to say?" After what seemed like an eternity, he opened his mouth, "You want to buy a camel?"

I excitedly said, "Yes!"

He said, "Okay, we have one camel for sale. Please come this way," and he led me around the circus wagons until we came to a large enclosure with camels in it. Pointing at one camel, he said, "This one we will sell."

In the past, I had tried to purchase animals from zoos, but they would not sell them. I thought of importing one, but I learnt that quarantine would cost a fortune. All my efforts to get a camel and add it to my animal collection had so far been unsuccessful. But here was a man right in front of me with his camel, saying, "We will sell it."

I heard all the bells ringing in my mind, warning: *Don't do it*. But I knew I was going for it. I was taking the camel home regardless of the cost involved. He told me the price, and we had a bit of a haggle, but finally, we came to an agreement. I told him that I would be coming the next day with the money and a horse box to carry the camel. He said, "Okay. No problem."

Soon, I was on my way back home, feeling very happy and overly excited. And another night passed without any sleep for me. While my entire household slept away, I kept awake thinking about riding this camel all around, dressed up maybe as an Arab. In my mind, I was already riding the camel down and around the town, and I felt so excited, like a wee boy with his first toy.

The next day, just before the bank opened, I was outside waiting to go in and withdraw the money. I had already asked my neighbour if I could borrow his recently bought horse box that could carry at least three horses, and he had said, 'Yes.'

Without wasting time, we were on our way to Dundalk with a huge horse box trailing behind our small car. On reaching the circus venue, I went straight to the boss's cabin and knocked on the door. The young circus manager came out with a smile, rubbing his hands. I handed him the money, and he ordered his men, "Go and get the camel."

After signing the ownership papers, I stood waiting impatiently for what felt like forever until I decided to walk in the direction where I had seen the men going earlier to bring the camel to me.

From around the corner, seven men appeared, walking backward like those in a tug-of-war game, pulling ropes similar to those used to secure a boat in a harbour. Inch by inch, they struggled backward, and then I saw it—a massive eight-foot-high monster of a camel that looked like it was possessed, roaring and spitting at the men who were trying to pull it toward the transport.

Chapter 14 - Discovering the Gift

The circumstances looked like something out of a circus, but instead of the camel being the show, the ringmaster was the camel, and the big burly men were the act.

I realised my thinking was wrong. I assumed the camel would be like a pony and that I could lead it around without any problem. You see, I knew about camels, but I did not *know* them. It had been that way all my life—thinking I understood their nature, but when the rubber hit the road, I knew nothing about them, especially this monster. The men had pulled the camel towards my horsebox, coaxing it with grain, apples, and everything they could think of just to get it inside.

Finally, after much pulling and pushing, they managed to get the camel into the box. When they got him in, the front of the horsebox went down, and the front of my car lifted into the air.

Nothing was going right. I looked at Thomas and sighed, "What am I going to do?" He looked at me and said, "I don't know, Daddy." With that childish innocence, he asked, "What are you going to do?" I mumbled, "We may take it home and shoot it."

The truth was, I was stuck with it, and I had to take it with me—home, or anywhere. I couldn't let my latest purchase stand idly and confused like its equally confused owner in the circus area any longer. We drove off at about twenty miles an hour, overloaded with this big monster that I was carrying home to my wife, who knew nothing about it. She had thought I was joking when I'd told her the previous night about buying a camel. All I wished now was to put the camel in a stable, shut the door, go to sleep, and wake up in the morning hoping *it was only just a weird dream.*

When we reached home, I used a jack to take the box off the car and hitched it onto the Land Rover. We took it around to the stable and spent nearly half an hour getting the camel out of the box. Myself,

Thomas, and my workers coaxed and pushed it toward the stable using the gates. We kept pushing, shoving, and pulling—anything to get this beast to move. Finally, we barely reached the stable door, and I looked up at the camel, then at the door, and back at the camel. "This monster is too big to go through the stable door," I realised—two feet too high. So close, yet so far. But there was just no way this monster was going to win. It *would* go through the door one way or another.

I found my sledgehammer and broke off all the cement above the door. Finally, we got her into the stable. If only it had ended there. Once inside, she raised her back, and her two humps lifted the entire roof off the stable. Nothing was going right. And the reason was simple; I *thought* I knew how camels were, but I knew nothing about them. I hadn't studied them at all, and that was glaringly obvious now. I would have to learn the hard way—through experience.

One day, I was on the opposite side of my home from where I kept the camel when a car came in, blasting loud music. Above every other noise, I could hear a heavy *bump, bump, bump* of the beat. My friend suddenly ran around the corner of the house, shouting, "John, John, come quickly!" Then, turning to run back the way he'd come, waving at me to follow, I didn't know what I was about to run into.

As I turned the corner, I was speechless—my mouth fell open. I stood there, amazed to see the camel, who had given me so much trouble, dancing on two legs… to the beat of the deafening music. After a few minutes, I shouted, "Switch off the music!" Behold, the camel stopped dancing. "Switch it on again!" I called out. The camel took off dancing once more. It was then I remembered she was a circus camel.

I would eventually learn everything I needed to know about having a camel, and it wasn't long before we developed an inseparable bond. I named her Camilla. She became my favourite animal friend and the star attraction among all the other animals. She presented herself as an imposing giant of an animal before her human "midgets." Strangers and visitors from far and near would flock to see her, marvelling at this seldom-seen creature of the desert.

John's son Thomas and grandson Israel

One day, Camilla escaped from her enclosure and wandered across the fields. She was spotted by many drivers and passengers travelling on the Dublin Road that day. Some of them were probably seeing a camel for the first time. Many people even stopped their cars to watch in amazement and take pictures of her roaming freely among the trees and in the open green fields. The authorities were alerted, and soon there was a helicopter hovering overhead and police cars dispatched. Finally, after five gruelling but exciting hours, Camilla was brought back from her short-lived adventure to her enclosure.

She blended seamlessly into her environment, her antics becoming a familiar and cherished sight along the Dublin Road. With her lively personality and distinctive appearance, she captured the attention of all who passed by. Full of life, her quirky movements and friendly interactions delighted locals and visitors alike. Over time, her popularity grew so much that even the media were drawn to my mini zoo, eager to capture her on camera and speak with me about her story.

People would highlight Camilla as part of the rural charm in Newry, showing how I cared for her and how she had become an integral part of our community. The BBC was one of the TV stations that featured her in a humorous and memorable report, showcasing her as a local celebrity. With the news coverage, her fame spread beyond Newry, making her a delightful topic for people across the region. Her story illustrated not only her endearing qualities but also the simple joy that unexpected animal encounters can bring to a community. Camilla remained a gentle and unusual resident, where visitors often caught glimpses of her "dancing" or playfully peeking out from her enclosure, bringing a touch of humour and novelty to their day.

When I look back on that time, I realise my understanding of camels was akin to my knowledge of hell. I thought I knew about hell and even made and shared hundreds of jokes about it, but I knew nothing. However, today, by the grace of God, I can say that I know better about both camels and hell. But I would not want anyone to ever get the shock that I got with the camel or with the reality of hell. The word "Hell" finds more mention than "Heaven" in the Bible. And there is no escape from it. It is not like going to prison for five or ten years and then coming out after serving your sentence. Once you go through the gates of hell, there is no way out whatsoever. You would be burning, screaming, and grinding your teeth forever. There would be no partying, no drugs, no drinks, and no messing about down in the fiery pit of hell. Once you are in, you are damned for eternity.

There is coming a day when each of our lives will be taken from our bodies, and we will be judged by God according to our deeds. It will be either Hell or Heaven for us. There will be nothing in between. It will either be Hell, where you will burn forever, or Heaven, where there will be no more tears or sorrows, only peace and happiness.

God wants you to be in Heaven with Him forever, but satan is out to rob your soul so that you may spend eternity with him in hell. If you reject Christ, you are in danger of losing your soul forever, and this is the truth. I used to joke and laugh about hell without realising the danger my soul was in. I had always carried a misguided notion that religion would help me get to Heaven or keep me from going to hell.

Today, I know that man-made religion can never get anyone to Heaven. Only Jesus Christ who can guide and lead us there. Jesus Christ alone can save us from hell. For every soul in this life, it is either going to be Heaven or Hell when the great Judgement Day comes. There is no 'in-between' and no middle road. God knew this, and He found a way for us to be reconciled with Him and gain access to Heaven through Jesus.

Heaven seems impossible when we realise that we have been born into a sinful world, with sin that has its root in the Garden of Eden. But God has made Heaven possible for us, sinners, through the sacrifice of His only begotten Son on the Cross. It is only by the blood of Jesus Christ that our sins can be forgiven. There is nothing in this whole world that can remove the stain of sin from your soul except the blood of Jesus. You cannot do it by yourself—only God can do it.

God can forgive you and transform you in ways unimaginable, and I know this because He forgave me and changed my life completely. People can try and change you but true change comes from the heart and God is the only one who can transform our heart. I share my story of victory in Him because I truly believe that you too can have victory in God and share the joy of salvation.

CHAPTER 15

God is Calling

For 32 years, whether a small or large group of people, I've shared God's Word in house meetings, churches, and conferences worldwide.

One thing that stood out among those meetings is when the people witness God moving and then discover that I cannot read or write. A common question arises: "How do you prepare yourself to allow God to flow through you?" My answer is simple, 'I go to the mountain.'

Most of you will know the story of Moses reaching the top of Mount Sinai. But what if Moses had stayed at the bottom of the Mountain? Would he have received the Ten Commandants? Or Peter; He had the choice of staying in the boat with the rest of his comrades, but in walking on water, he had a testimony none of the others had. And there are many more… Noah, David, Samson, Paul, etc. Each one of them had a choice and in choosing God, they chose to have a God-life experience.

How did they cross that line from natural life to God-life?

They did it through obedience and death to self; in other words, it is not my will, but God's will[9] done through me.

---

[9] John 6:38.

God's will comes through obedience—listening to and doing what He says. It takes place through death to self. In other words, when we could be doing other things, we climb the mountain towards love and worship.

The Secret Place—Discovered

I am like the rest of you. I have a family, work, and commitments. But each day I choose which one would be the most important in my life for that day. I consider all demands for my time and then I choose God first. I would go to the mountain near my home, park the vehicle in the car park at the bottom, and then start my walk.

You see a lot of my inspiration comes when I pray on the mountain—a secret place to me. It's where I go to commune with God, listen, and obey.

Mountains are more than just physical landscapes; they are sanctuaries where one can engage in deep communion with God. This sacred space provides a unique opportunity for reflection, insight, and inspiration essential for preaching and guiding others. By seeking solitude in the mountains, I draw closer to the divine and emerge equipped to share God's love and wisdom with the world.

Listen carefully, 'Where is your mountain?' Oh, I'm not speaking entirely of a real mountain. As many of you reading this book may not even have a mountain near you. Or some cannot climb so what do you do?

The Mountain is what the Bible calls our Secret Place.

The Secret Place is not so much the earthly location—if it were, Jesus would have stayed in one spot. But He never stopped entering His Secret Place. Listen carefully and this is the truth, The Secret Place is our heart's location. Can I ask, "Have you attended to yours?"

In a world overflowing with noise and distraction, the Secret Place offers peace and refuge from the tumult of everyday life. My act of going to the mountains to commune with God is a pilgrimage that transcends my physical journey; it embodies a spiritual quest for clarity, strength, and a deeper understanding of the purpose of my life.

In the fast-paced modern world, finding moments of solitude is increasingly rare. The mountains offer me an escape from the noise of daily life, allowing for deep soul-searching and inspection. Alone in nature, I can reflect on personal experiences, struggles, and aspirations. This solitude creates a fertile ground for my spiritual growth. The stillness invites prayer, meditation, and listening—which is crucial in speaking with God.

During this reflective time, I could be confronted with profound questions: What is my purpose? How can I serve others more effectively? What messages does God wish for me to share? As the mind quiets, answers often emerge with clarity and conviction. This process of reflection not only strengthens my faith, but also equips me for the days ahead.

My retreat to the mountains is not merely an end but a spur for action. The inspiration gleaned from the divine encounter compels me to return to my community with a renewed sense of purpose. Whether through acts of service, compassionate outreach, or the simple sharing of my faith story, the journey encourages me to live out my convictions in tangible ways.

The people I meet along the mountain trails also offer me invaluable life lessons. On one particular walk, a young lady inspired me, "What we take for granted, others can truly appreciate." She took a close-up photograph of the top of my walking stick, carved in the shape of an elephant's head. She appreciated the work that it entailed, while I appreciated the strength of it, holding me up. If she could take a moment to admire the work of hands that transformed a piece of wood into an elephant's head, surely, we too, should take time to recognise and appreciate the beauty of God's workmanship all around us with thanksgiving in our hearts.

The Bible states over 30 times, *"Give thanks unto the Lord."* You know by now I didn't go to school but surely, if the teacher told me something 30 times, either I am not listening or I am not seeing it as important.

I have learnt to 'Give thanks to the Lord,' and it all started, not just by learning about praise in the Bible, but by acknowledging my surroundings.

Look around you and see what is there ... a home, family, car, pet and so forth. Then look around more and see the flowers, how they grow from nothing into beauty, see the majestic mountains, feel the wind in your face, and thank God. Look around, and thank God for the small things in life.

There I stood on the mountain appreciating who God is, and what He has done for me; those who have been in my life even to the smallest flower budding, "I thank you God for your beauty."

One day there were two ladies walking past me and I asked them, "Do you know the gardener?"

They looked at each other and realised I must be asking about the person who was the caretaker of the mountain, they said, "No, do you?"

"Yes" I said it's Jesus, and with that, I shared with them that when one walks through a castle garden, they see lovely shrubs on display, all laid out by man. It has been done for the visitors' eyes. Then there is the greatest Gardener, called our glorious Saviour Jesus Christ. He has laid out the beauty of this world so that we can appreciate His wonders. They looked around where they stood as if it was the first time they ever saw it, and as the gazed I heard them say, "Your right, your right."

As I left them in deep thought, I heard a car horn tooting and a couple were trying to draw my attention. They jumped out of their car and met me as I walked over to them. I greeted them and noticed they were not locals by their accents. "Where are you from?" I asked. They answered politely, "America." Then I continued, "What brings you here?" They said, "It is our first time in Ireland and we are lost."

Then they asked, "Are you out for a walk?" My answer was, "Yes and no. You see this is where I come to spend time with the Lord Jesus and I was about to go back down the mountain when I heard you tooting at me."

"Oh, we are sorry to disturb you. Are you a reverend?" "Yes," I responded. They continued, "We've just got engaged" and looking into each other's eyes asked, "Could you bless our engagement?" There, we joined hands and I prayed over them.

As I prayed, I saw a flock of geese flying overhead in a V formation, and the Lord impressed upon my heart to share this: even the fowl of the air know where they are going.

"You see those geese above our heads?" I asked. "When they were born in a shell, no one showed them a map of where to go in life; but at no point do we ever hear of geese being lost. Those geese you are seeing leave here each year and have pitstops in Greenland and Iceland, before finishing up in Canada—they know their destination. Now, did you ever ask, how do they know that there is even a pitstop once they have started to fly out into the sea? How do they know what direction to go in?" The couple just looked at each other as if to say,

'Go on, tell us more.' "The answer is, there is something built into them. It's a sense of survival, of going to the next stage in their life. Like a swimmer knowing they have to come up again for air, God has put a compass in our spirit that only seeks to draw us to Him.

You arrived here lost, but in reality, you were found. With all of your being, you can say, "I was lost but now I am found!""

Let me ask you reader. Surely, if God can put a compass into an animal, how much more of a compass has He put in you? You see, if those geese did not listen to their heart compass, they would never see the world that is waiting for them. Likewise, it is the same with each sinner. God has a place called Heaven waiting for us. We may have pitstops of life, but all in all, we are on a path either to Heaven or to hell, depending on how our compass has been set.

Now, you have a chance to reset your compass, have it pointed towards Heaven, and have our lovely Saviour's arms carry you until you reach your final destination.

CHAPTER 16

Do You Meet the Requirements?

The story of every true believer ends with a hope of Heaven, where we will spend eternity with our Lord. And I would like to conclude my book with the truth of my Eternal Home where I shall live after my journey on earth comes to an end. We know that hell is real, and life is not a game. We also know that none of us is going to live forever. There will come a day when each one of us will be taken from this earth. Every one of us knows of somebody who has already gone before us. So, we know our bus is also coming in soon, at our appointed time. Wouldn't it be nice to know what bus you are getting on? But, in the same breath, wouldn't it be terrible if you hop on to the wrong bus? When we ask Jesus into our lives, we know our destination. The question is, do you know yours?

I want you to imagine Heaven. When you enter Heaven, you will see people that have come from all over the world; they have entered their eternal home—to be with Jesus.

There will be Noah, sharing about how his Father in Heaven gave him the vision to build the ark. David, sharing about the day he took a block of cheese to his brothers in the Israel army, to only hear and see Goliath standing mocking God. We know how the story goes… Then there is Rahab, chatting to Joshua about how they stepped into God, and I could go on and on. But what I would like to know, 'Will you have a story to share when you enter those gates about how you walked with Jesus?'

You see my friend, everyone in Heaven will have a story. A story that will glorify their Saviour Jesus Christ; of how they listened to Him and overcame every obstacle that stood in their way. By faith we overcome.

As the Bible says, *"Without faith it is impossible to please God."* I ask of you, reach out your heart to God in faith, He has wonderful plan for you.

All I ask is that you pray the following prayer with me that I have prayed on behalf of thousands of people whom I have led to the Lord; may Heaven hear you say it.

> **"Oh Lord Jesus, I know that I am a sinner and I ask You to forgive me for my sins. I open the door of my heart and welcome You in. Come in, Lord Jesus, come in to stay. Change my life, Your way, according to Your will. I thank You, Lord Jesus, for dying for me, and I thank You, Lord, for saving me." Amen.**

The Bible says, *"That if you confess with your mouth Jesus as Lord, and believe in your heart that God raised Him from the dead, you will be saved."* (Romans 10:9).

Once you have prayed that prayer the blood of Jesus will cleanse your heart and soul resetting your inner compass that will start to draw you to His will for your life. As you listen to His voice, and when He speaks—obey, for there is no other way.

As I draw my book to a close, tears are in my eyes. They are tears of love—God's love for you, yes, you. If this book is worth anything, let it be the bridge that draws you to Christ.

Chapter 16 - Do You Meet the Requirements?

John's sketch for his Heaven and Hell message

I mean this with all my heart. There would be nothing more I would hold dear than to know you have accepted Christ as your loving Saviour or have recommitted your life to Him and you never know, someday we could finish this chat in Heaven.

***

Let me finish with one last story.

For my mission to America, I had planned to bring my daughter Melissa along. We had booked our meetings three months in advance, set to take place in Arizona, New Mexico, and California. I was also scheduled to preach to the Native Americans who live on reservations. With a lot of travel ahead, I started gathering all the necessary documents. That's when I noticed that my passport was due to expire in a month. In case you aren't aware, a passport must be valid for at least three months before its expiry date to travel. Panic set in as I told Patricia that my American trip might have to be cancelled because I needed to renew my passport.

Patricia suggested I go right away to get a new photo and passport application. So, I got myself dressed up in a shirt and tie, combed my hair, and put on some aftershave—not sure how that would help the photo, but I figured it couldn't hurt! Off to Newry town I went.

I remembered the shopping centre had one of those photo kiosks and thought it would do the trick. I sat down in the booth, put the money in, and waited—FLASH!—the whole cubicle lit up, practically blinding me. Nervously, I waited for the photos to print, and out they came. To this day, I remember looking at them and saying out loud, "That's not me—I'm better looking than that!" Blaming the machine, I decided I needed to upgrade the camera.

Chapter 16 - Do You Meet the Requirements?

I found a photo studio and, with a hopeful smile, told the owner I needed a passport photo. His assistant took my picture, and I waited to see the results. She soon came out from the back room and handed me four prints. I thanked her, paid, and left the studio, eagerly anticipating my new photo for the next ten years. Once in the car, I opened the envelope, and I'm not sure if "appalled" is a strong enough word. I had never seen a worse photograph of myself. Out loud, I muttered, "What's wrong with these cameras?" There was no way I could put such an image on my passport.

Determined, I visited another photographer, making sure my hair, tie, and appearance were all perfect. When I received the next set of photos, they were even worse than the first. Frustrated, I wondered what I would do with all these unflattering pictures. Then I remembered a new photo shop seven miles from town. Surely, being new, their camera would produce a better image. Once again, I had my picture taken, telling myself this would be the last attempt, no matter the outcome. But when I looked at the result, it was worse than the others. Resigned, I went home, feeling less confident in my appearance than ever.

I showed the photos to my wife, saying with an unhappy face, "That's not me." She looked at the photos, then at me, and replied, "That is you. Pick one and send it." I couldn't bring myself to choose, so I threw them onto the table and said, "You pick one and send it off." And that's exactly what she did.

Now, there was good and bad news regarding my passport.

The good news was; my passport arrived in time for travel. The bad news? Patricia had picked the worst of the photos, and so for the next few years, I'd have to look at a passport picture of someone who wasn't as good-looking as me.

The time came and we drove to the airport and boarded a large plane bound for America. During the flight, we met some American Christians who, upon learning about my mission to preach—including to Native American communities—shared insights about the vast lands on the reservations. Our conversation made the long journey enjoyable and helped pass the time quickly.

When we landed, Melissa and I followed our new friends to the immigration queue. As we got closer to the officer checking each passport, I could hear him saying, "Go ahead, go ahead" after each passenger. When my turn came, I handed over my passport. The officer looked at it, then at me, and said, "Sir, you are an alien."

Confused, the only alien I knew was ET, whom I'd seen on screen. Bewildered, I replied, "Sir, I know it's not a great photo, but I don't understand." The officer repeated, "Sorry, sir, you're an alien. You're holding up the line." Still baffled, I asked for clarification. He explained, "Sir, you're a visitor to our country. This line is for American citizens," and pointed to another line marked for visitors from different nationalities. Realising my mistake, Melissa and I moved to the correct line and were soon in the land of the free.

Years later, I would look back at that photograph I once disliked, surprised by how youthful and handsome I appeared back then. Today, after life's wear and tear, I realise I looked much better than I do now!

The experience taught me that every country has an entry point, and one must meet the gatekeepers' requirements to enter. I thank God that, through His Son Jesus, He gave us the ability to meet the requirements to enter Heaven.

I pray that we all will meet God's requirements, and enter through those gates. Who knows? I might tell you another story up there.

To contact the author

Email: office@JohnPurcell.co.uk

To invite John to minister or purchase his books visit

www.JohnPurcell.co.uk

Inspired to write a book?

Contact

Maurice Wylie Media
Your Inspirational & Christian Book Publisher
Based in Northern Ireland and distributing around the world

www.MauriceWylieMedia.com

www.ingramcontent.com/pod-product-compliance
Lightning Source LLC
Chambersburg PA
CBHW041142110526
44590CB00027B/4098